The
Kennedy Women

The
Kennedy Women

A PERSONAL APPRAISAL

PEARL S. BUCK

BY ARRANGEMENT WITH
THE JOHN DAY COMPANY · NEW YORK

COWLES BOOK COMPANY, INC.

NEW YORK

Photograph credits (in order of appearance)
Stanley Tretick, LOOK; Bradford Bachrach; Stanley Tretick, LOOK;
UPI; Douglas Jones, LOOK; Stanley Tretick, LOOK; Stanley Tretick,
LOOK; James Hansen, LOOK; Stanley Tretick, LOOK; Stanley Tretick,
LOOK; Stanley Tretick, LOOK; Stanley Tretick, LOOK; Stanley Tretick,
LOOK; Douglas Jones, LOOK; Stanley Tretick, LOOK; Stanley Tretick,
LOOK; Stanley Tretick, LOOK; Stanley Tretick, LOOK; Stanley Tretick,
LOOK; Wide World.

The
Kennedy Women

1

IN THE middle of the night on July 18, 1969, Edward Kennedy's car veered and fell over the edge of a narrow bridge on a country road into the dark deep water below. He was not alone. A young woman, Mary Jo Kopechne, was with him and she drowned.

Is this a curse — the curse that has haunted all the Kennedys?

The tragedy was not a simple one. No tragedy that befalls a great family can ever be simple. The hold of a family of power upon society is always complex and profound, complex because the family tentacles reach deeply into the life of the society; profound, because the imagination of every member of the society is quickened by the power, the grace and disgrace, the glory and the shame of the family. It is so in the United States, it was so in China where also I belong.

I remember the famous Kung family who lived in the *hutung* next to mine in Peking. I knew them, but everyone knew them, if not face to face, then rumor to rumor. There were three sons and two daughters. The daughters married sons of rich men, the sons married the daughters of rich men, and a curse lay upon them all.

The youngest son was killed by his own father as a duty to the family. In those days in China a family, and certainly a great family, was responsible for every member of the family, although when a daughter married she became the responsibility of her husband's family, as sons' wives became the responsibility of the sons' family.

Was it possible that the last, dearest son of the Kung family in Peking could die by his father's hand? It was possible because it so happened. Everyone knew the trouble this honored family had with its youngest son. He had disobeyed his tutor when he was a child. As a boy in his teens he stole out of the house at night, aided by conniving servants, and joined in the acts of street rowdies. No one cared what the street rowdies did, but everyone cared what a son of the Kung family did. He was heartlessly blamed, he was ruthlessly criticized, and because he was a Kung he could not be forgiven.

But the boy himself also had greatness. Whatever he did, in evil or in good, he outdid all others. He was incorrigible. When his father perceived that, for the sake of the family and society he acted as honor compelled him to do. After explaining the necessity to his son, the tears running down his cheeks as he did so, he took a small pistol from the drawer of the teakwood table beside which he sat in his usual carved armchair and, with quick and accurate aim, he killed his son.

This, in another age and country, was acclaimed an act befitting the father of a great family. I heard cries of admiration on every side. The father had not hesitated to do his duty to the people, the Old Hundred Names. The Kung family remained inviolate in its position.

But I, always curious and rebellious, went to visit my friends, the women, taking with me restorative fruits and sweets suitable for the occasion. I wanted to see how deep this sense of family honor penetrated into the heart of the family, the women. Did they approve—nay, could they ever endure what had been done?

I was received quietly and with dignity. Many times I had been a guest in the Kung household, but never under such tragic circumstance. All was as usual on the surface. Each daughter, each daughter-in-law, was in her place and at her duty, though each wore a sign of mourning, a cord of white in the knot of her hair, or white cotton cloth sewed over her shoes, or a white cotton skirt, for in those days Chinese ladies still wore pleated skirts instead of the tight long gowns of today's women.

We did not mention the tragedy when Madame

Kung received me in the great hall. Instead we talked of small events such as the lotus in the courtyard pool, the season being summer, or the stumbling first steps of a grandchild, a serving maid supporting him by a strip of cloth about his middle. At last, however, a silence fell and endured so long that I looked at Madame Kung and saw that she was weeping. When she observed my notice, she wiped her eyes and controlled herself.

"We are a family ancient and great," she said. "What we have learned we know very well."

"What is it you know?" I asked.

She replied with quiet resignation. "We know that greatness always carries with it a curse. Cursed are the mighty, for the gods and men combine against them to bring them low." I remember now that conclusion. I know now its meaning and its truth.

In the heart and mind of the common man, the common woman, the average child, a basic fear arouses a natural hatred of the unusual, the talented, the brilliant, the innovator. This hatred is mingled at the same time with an unwilling "love," an envious admiration.

It is as true in my own country, among my own people, in my own times and experience, as it was with the Kung family half a century ago, when I was a young woman. Time does not change the essential nature of man. So it has always been, throughout human history. The human race owes all progress, all knowledge, to the few truly gifted, the outstanding ones. Yet it persecutes its saviors.

Remembering the Kung family of my youth, I survey my present scene, to ponder upon its modern American counterpart: the Kennedy family.

The roots of this very modern family are in Ireland, not ancient, not growing slowly and deeply through many centuries as the Kungs did, but swiftly, strongly, almost suddenly, through a strong central figure, the father.

My natural interest in this American family is, of course, what it was in the Chinese family, the women. I repeat, the heart of any family is to be found in the women, and first among the women, the mother. Yet one cannot know the mother until one knows the woman she was before she became the mother.

———•—◆—◆—•———

Rose Fitzgerald Kennedy grew up in luxury as the daughter of a successful political figure in Boston, John F. Fitzgerald, nicknamed Honey Fitz. Her mother was a quiet, home-loving woman, much like Madame Kung on the other side of the world, so home-loving, indeed, that she did not enjoy the public gatherings her husband loved, and her daughter Rose often took her place as hostess.

Consider the value of this contrast in parents for a beautiful, intelligent young girl! She learned to understand and love the ebullient, rollicking, irrepressible father, she could even be amused by his propensity for singing "Sweet Adeline," on all occasions, and certainly early she learned the wisdom of allowing a man to be himself, whatever that was.

But her real life was at home with her mother, a life almost conventional in its activities. She went to St. John's School in the North End of Boston, she lived near Codman's Square in Dorchester where she graduated at the age of fifteen from public school, and her father, who was then mayor, proudly handed her the diploma she well deserved, for she was a good student. She went then to the Sacred Heart Convent School on Commonwealth Avenue in Boston's aristocratic Back Bay and afterward to Manhattanville College in New York. Still later she attended a German convent finishing school in Holland, and in those quiet and beautiful surroundings she learned the serenity and love of peace which have been so characteristic of her ever since.

She came back again as the elder daughter, beautiful and beloved, to the comfortable Boston home. There, acting as her father's hostess in his vivid and forceful political life, she found time for her own life, too. She and her sister, Agnes, taught catechism classes in the North End, they worked in welfare organizations, but they also helped their father in his obligations to important people, acting as translators for German and French delegates to the International Congress their father had encouraged. So proud was this father of his beautiful daughter Rose that once on his way south to Palm Beach he actually stopped off in Washington to introduce her to President William McKinley.

And yet this beautiful girl learned early to accept and deal with fate as it attacked. She was Irish and in conservative old Boston society the Irish were intruders. When Rose applied for membership to the Junior League, she was refused. Did she accept the refusal meekly? She did not. She formed her own organization, the Ace of Clubs, which became as exclusive as the Junior League. She began the Travel Club, she became president of the Lenox Club and belonged to other organizations in whose work she was interested. Never were the clubs purely social. She had a serious depth in her nature, and if her interest were to be caught and held, it must be by some useful purpose. She was therefore an interesting combination of her humor-loving father and her quiet, home-loving mother.

With all this, she was also glamorous, and many men loved her. Her debut into Irish society was talked about as an affair unique in its glitter, with four hundred and fifty of Boston's rich young men and women. Among the men who, it was said, asked to marry her was the Englishman Sir Thomas Lipton, yachtsman, tea merchant, and her father's friend. Today Rose scoffs at the mention of this, but she smiles as she scoffs, as though savoring a secret joke.

She chose fiery, red-haired Joseph P. Kennedy, a youthful banker who stood at the start of an enormously successful financial career. He had already gained control of the Columbia Trust Company in East Boston and, at twenty-five, had become the youngest bank president in Massachusetts.

In spite of this he was no favorite of her father, who opposed the marriage. When Joe put the engagement ring on her finger, he did so as they stood together on the sidewalk. Her father, Honey Fitz, would not let him into the house.

My knowledge of Madame Kung helps me understand Rose Kennedy. The two women are very different and yet they are basically alike. Even their personal names are different. Madame Kung's "small name" was Jade Orchid — jade so cool, orchid so exquisite but without scent. Rose? There is color in a rose, and the scent, however delicate, is always unmistakably the rose. Both women are ladies, although the Kung family can trace its lineage directly back to the great Confucius, who lived five hundred years before Christ, and the Kennedy family left its native Ireland little more than a hundred years ago.

———— ·•·•·•· ————

In 1849 Patrick Joseph Kennedy left the village of New Ross in County Wexford, Ireland, and took ship in the port of Cork for America. It was the year of the great famine, caused by five years of potato blight. The Irish starved as Chinese starved when a basic crop failed. True, the Kungs had never starved, for their family had lasted in its greatness for many centuries, and the Kennedy family was new. Yet there must have been a power in Patrick Joseph, for many like him died in the filthy, crowded steerage of cheap packet ships. But Patrick lived to land on Noddle's Island, a part of Boston, and there he found his new world.

It was a world different indeed from that of the Kung family in Peking. The counterpart of Patrick Joseph was old Mr. Kung, the grandfather of the Chinese house, very old, very elegant, very remote. I dared not speak to him when I passed him on my way to the women's quarters of the Kung family. He sat in summertime in the shade of a date tree in the courtyard and a slave girl fanned him gently, her palm-leaf fan moving slowly to and fro. Most of the time old Mr. Kung's eyes were closed, but sometimes as I passed he opened them and I saw they were narrow and dead, like the eyes of a lizard.

He was too old to care who passed, but I had heard stories of his youth and I knew his eyes had not always been like that. In his day he had been handsome and impetuous and strong, the Chinese counterpart of Patrick Joseph Kennedy. There was one great difference between them, however. Mr. Kung came into a family long established in an ancient country. Patrick Joseph came, brash, new, and unknown, into a brash, new country strange to him. And he came to Boston, where an Irishman was all but the lowest among its citizens. "The Irish are all right as long as they know their place," a Bostonian said. And everyone in Boston knew what that place was.

Yet, far apart in time and space, these two men had qualities in common. Both men were courageous, both were innovators. Patrick Joseph came to a new country; Mr. Kung helped to create a new country from an old one. He became a secret rebel against the Manchu dynasty then ruling China, for he saw that unless his beloved country modernized, it could not stand against the imperialistic West. He was among the handful of men who penetrated the palace and persuaded the young Emperor to work in secret against the imperious, powerful old Empress Dowager, Tzu Hsi.

When their plot was discovered and the young Emperor was murdered, old Mr. Kung, young and still rebellious, was saved only because of the influence of his family. But the family was compelled to promise that never again would he be permitted to leave the family courtyards, and never again did he do so. From his lizard eyes, he saw life pass him by, a figure of tragedy. Yet he did not yield.

He was a scholar, and when he could find a westerner to teach him English, he employed him. With this new knowledge, he translated in secret those books of the West which had produced the modern age. Darwin and Marx, Shakespeare and Dickens, hundreds of books he translated under an assumed name, and thousands of young men read them. From his courtyard prison, within the shelter of his great family, Mr. Kung maintained his invincible way.

Across the sea in the slums of Boston, U.S.A., Patrick Joseph Kennedy was founding his own great family in the same invincible way. He was only twenty-six years old, and he had become an expert barrel maker. He was luckier than most of his fellows. Since he had a decent trade, he was able to escape the cruel exploitation Irish Catholics usually suffered. Newspaper help-wanted advertisements frequently carried the warning "No Irish Need Apply."

He married a strong, good Irishwoman and with her had three daughters. But, like his Chinese counterpart, he longed for a son, and in 1858 the son was born, a new Patrick. Alas, before the family had time to become great, the first Patrick, the father, died. The mother, Bridget Murphy, kept the children together, and the second Patrick eventually had a son whom his wife, Mary Hickey, named Patrick, too. But she reversed the two names, not wanting her son to be a junior to his father, and so Joseph Patrick Kennedy took his place in the making of a great American family, merely by being born.

East and West, the basic strength of both families lay in the qualities of strength and courage.

They were not afraid of new ventures. They were innovators, and they were determined to have their way. Somehow, they had it.

I believe it takes a strong woman to marry a strong man. Strong women do not, as a rule, marry weak men. If they do, the marriage does not last, or is not a happy one. The maternal instinct in women is much overrated. There is, of course, a period in any woman's life, or almost any woman's, when she wants to be a mother. At least, she wants to have a child, and, having a child, she is perforce a mother. But the period passes and eventually she wants to get on with her own life. She does not want to have a husband who regards her as a mother. Perhaps the root of the trouble between man and woman in the United States is that the man expects his wife to be also his mother, while the wife wants her husband to be a man only. A wise woman chooses a man who is a man.

When Rose Fitzgerald stood on the sidewalk to let Joseph Patrick Kennedy put an engagement ring on her finger, she was already a strong woman, ready to defy her powerful father, but she defied him quietly, for she had learned the strength of quietness from her mother. There is no force on earth so indomitable, so unbreakable, as the force of a quiet woman who knows what she wants and is determined to have it.

Rose had known Joseph Patrick from childhood. Her family and his went to the same resort in summer. Her father, John, was a politician, as was Joseph Patrick's father, Pat Kennedy. If Joseph did not notice the slim pretty girl, it was only because he was still too young — too young and too busy. He was too busy being the captain of his team, whatever the team happened to be.

"Remember," he would say to his brothers and sisters, "if you can't be captain, don't play."

It was the slogan for his life. He applied it for a time to his school life. But in time he did not see schooling as "profitable." Busy as he was, and he had a clear eye for the making of a dollar, he wanted to drop out of school. But a teacher who saw the boy's promise persuaded the parents not to allow it. Back to school he went, while Rose was earning high marks in her convent school, and on to Harvard he went, earning five thousand dollars running a sightseeing bus during vacations, while he flunked a course in finance.

When college was over, he set himself to making money, not only in one venture but in several. While Rose was acting as her father's hostess and had become the leading young beauty of Boston's Irish society, Joseph Patrick was learning how to make money and manage it. He was determined to be rich and to live in a fine house in luxury such as the Cabots had and the Lodges. He worked long days at his desk in shirt sleeves, but when he left the office he wore a banker's conservative suit, a Homburg hat, and a grave face. Under this exterior, he cultivated a hard heart, or thought he did. He learned how to foreclose a mortgage, how to drive a bargain. He wanted to be rich.

In October, 1914, when in Europe armies were marching to what was to be a world war, Rose Fitzgerald was married to Joseph Patrick Kennedy.

2

WHAT manner of woman was Rose Kennedy now? She was beautiful to look at.
I put beauty, physical beauty, as God's first gift to woman. With beauty, her battles are easily won; without beauty, she has to contrive. Beauty gives her the basic self-confidence she needs. Beauty carries her through crises. With beauty she knows she can get her way, can achieve her ambitions, can arrive at her goals. She will be forgiven if she is beautiful. A woman cannot fail if she has beauty — that is, she cannot unless she destroys herself deliberately or through ignorance and folly. She may not have the love of women if she is too beautiful, but she will have the love of men, and that will serve her better. Moreover, her beauty is as good as a dowry to her husband. He will exhibit her with pride. Observe his good fortune, his good taste! He

has acquired something as valuable as jewels, and he need never be ashamed or apologetic. Other men will envy him.

Rose Kennedy had more than beauty, however. Her public life as her father's hostess had taught her self-possession, a surface of calm and composure. Like her mother, she did not seek public occasions, but when they came she knew how to present herself with dignity and a pleasant naturalness of behavior. No one could treat her casually, yet no one could think her cold. Underneath that lovely exterior, always chic, always appropriate, always quiet, there was a self-respect so absolute that it was self-willed. She could accept men and women as they were, demanding nothing, expecting nothing, as she observed, as she weighed, for she had everything.

This detachment, I think, was expressed even toward her husband, for it implied also a unique understanding of the impetuous, generous, yet hard-bargaining man she had married. Let it not be forgotten that she herself was a daughter of Ireland, and she knew that mercurial, hotheaded, witty, and irrepressible compound. She did not doubt for a moment that her husband would succeed in becoming someday a very rich, and therefore a very powerful, man.

In the United States money is power and there is no substitute. Like it or not, she knew the necessity of power, if her husband was to be a happy man. She did not, then, inquire into her husband's business.

Even in 1933, when the Senate Banking and Currency Committee called an investigation of a financial pool he was overseeing, so great were its profits, she asked no questions. She busied herself with her home and with the children who came quickly, one after the other. In three years she bore two sons, Joseph and John.

Now Rose Kennedy had reason to follow her mother's example and live her life in her home. While her husband devoted himself to his new job as general manager of Bethlehem Steel Fore River shipyard and to realizing his goal to make a million dollars while he was young enough to enjoy it, Rose devoted herself to her children. She was deeply and simply religious, not only on Sundays but as a profound and vital part of her life.

I had seen the same faith in religion when I came to know Madame Kung. The Chinese mother went to a Buddhist temple to pray: the American went to a cathedral, but there were amazing similarities. Images of gods and saints were in both temple and cathedral, and, while there was no cross in the temple, there was a virgin in each place of worship, a kindly Kwanyin, goddess of mercy, in the temple, and Mary the Virgin in the cathedral. Each lady, East and West, lit candles for her prayers, and each went to Mass, one Buddhist, one Christian.

I know Madame Kung could never have borne the weight of her large family and the troubled times unless she had gone daily to the temple; the

American mother, too, goes daily to the cathedral, to pray. Each gains strength from her own faith. I see the effect of this faith made manifest in the quiet stamina each possesses under the stress of tragedy.

Each has lost beloved sons. Madame Kung lost two of her three male children to the calculated fury of communism, and Rose Kennedy three sons, two to that strange, unreasoning fury against the great, the successful, which seems endemic in a democracy such as ours. Madame Kung's husband is dead also, a victim to the anger of his own unruly peasants, but the American woman had her own cross to bear in the living death of her beloved husband. How well I know the weight of that cross! It is a weight I, too, carried.

And yet she has another cross to carry, this beautiful American woman. Among her many children, four sons and five daughters, one daughter, the eldest, remains forever a child. How shall I write of *this* cross? I myself have had to bear it for many an endless year. I know all too well the horror of the doctor's decision, "Madame, your child is hopelessly retarded." How well I know that heart-sickening experience! It was once said to me after I had given birth to such a dear yet stricken baby daughter.

At first Rose could not believe it. She had given birth to two handsome, healthy sons; was it possible that this little girl child could be different? It was possible. It was a shattering reality. Rose Kennedy had produced a human being who could not fulfill herself, a waste, one would say. Except that in Rose Kennedy's life it has not been a waste. It has been a blessing to thousands of other children so afflicted, a comfort to thousands of heartbroken parents.

"It used to be so difficult for me to talk about Rosemary," Rose once said. "I just could not bring myself to do it years ago. But I wanted people to know it should be talked about, not hidden. That there is hope now."

There are two ways of bearing a cross, especially the cross of a retarded child. Some upon whom the cross falls cry out against God. Why, they demand, must this fate be theirs? What have they done to deserve the tragedy of a hopelessly retarded child? In resentment and anger, they take revenge upon the child. They banish the child from their sight. They thrust the child as early as possible into an institution, depriving the innocent one of the family love that every child deserves; they try to forget that the child was ever born.

There are others, however, who take up the cross bravely and live with its burden. They include the child in their lives. They make the child's life meaningful to the family, the community, the world. Rose Kennedy is one of these.

19

Her retarded daughter was not put aside or hidden. She was kept in the home and warmly loved by the family. And it was the mother who infused the love. In a home, in a family, everything depends upon the mother, especially when tragedy falls. If her spirit is rebellious and small, she influences every member adversely. They catch her attitudes and moods. They complain as she complains. They rebel with her rebellion, however futile it may be so to do.

Rose Kennedy was not one of these. She was already tempered by life, if not yet the demands of this experience. She was intelligent enough to be wise. She was sustained by her religion. God's will was her fate. There was a core of strength in her, an unshakable calm. Of course she shed tears. Of that I am certain. All mothers weep beneath that cross.

She once said, "Emotionalism in front of people is a sign of immaturity." But I am certain that she shed tears in private, as I did, and I am certain that she dried her eyes alone and then returned to her family and, with a beautiful new tenderness, she showed them by her example how to treat the helpless one among them.

When the time came, when Rosemary was twenty-one, she was put into a pleasant place, St. Coletta's school for exceptional children near Jefferson, Wisconsin, where she has companions of her own kind and is given gentle care. Such a time comes when the competition of normal people, even of loving brothers and sisters, becomes too bewildering for the one who has reached the limit of her development. But this was not the reach of her influence. Her family then put her life to use for others.

Small people, fearful people, people uncertain of their own worth, of their place in society, people afraid of what others think, would early have closed the doors of the institution upon the defective child.

Not so with the Kennedys. They fear nothing and no one. They need not consider the opinions of others. They need no approbation and fear no disapproval. They do what they wish and will. They announced the cross they bore, they sought out others who bore such a cross, they later, in 1946, after the death of their first son, established the Joseph P. Kennedy, Jr., Foundation, an organization to benefit the retarded. They changed the public atmosphere toward America's millions of mental retardees.

Behind all this was Rose Kennedy. In doing what she did, in accepting this first great tragedy as she did, she strengthened her own soul and prepared herself thereby for other tragedies to come.

Thinking of this woman, maintaining her resolute calm under the weight of cruel circumstance, I am reminded again of Madame Kung and her youngest and most dearly loved son. I remember him very well, that wildly rebellious little boy, ungovernable, unreachable, it seemed, by love or remonstrance or punishment. Something was wrong with him, of course. I am sure of it, in the light of much I have learned here in my own country. He was, doubtless, a psychopathic personality, one of those beings who, in spite of normal intelligence, sometimes even brilliant intelligence, seem to have no moral sense whatever and are therefore unteachable.

Of the two women, Rose Kennedy and Madame Kung, I felt that the Chinese mother's cross was the heavier. But a cross is still a cross, and the two women learned fortitude and acceptance. I do not use the word resignation, for that word carries with it a connotation of passivity and neither of these ladies was — or is — passive. They maintain their central position in the two great families they represent. They, and their families, are the greater for the tragedy that has befallen them.

———

What manner of mother was Rose Kennedy in those years when her children were growing up? She was a good wife and her husband was the head of the house. In this she was like Madame Kung. However the Chinese lady may have pleaded with her husband in private, whatever the tears she undoubtedly shed privately, in the presence of the family, and in public, Mr. Kung had his way, and she supported him.

In the twenties Joseph P. Kennedy had moved his family out of his native Boston because of the intolerable discrimination against Catholics as well as those of Irish descent. The father taught his lively brood that it was a privilege to be a Kennedy, and privilege carried obligations. They had responsibilities toward each other, toward their parents, their community, their country, even to the world. While the father was the driving leader, Rose, the mother, was the gentle upholder.

Both parents were exacting although in different ways. The father demanded punctuality at meals, the mother saw to it that there was punctuality. It was she, moreover, who took them to Mass every Sunday at St. Aidan's although she went alone every day for her own spiritual sustenance. And when the family sat together at the dinner table on Sunday, she asked questions about the sermon and the service. She was teacher as well as mother, and among the many lessons she taught, the most important, perhaps, was respect for the man who was head of the house. At home and in public she made gracefully apparent that her position was second to his, and in so doing enhanced her own personality.

Was she a housewife? Not in the ordinary sense. There was no need for her to be. Her husband had survived the 1929 financial crash with little loss. In the 1932 presidential campaign, he became one of Franklin D. Roosevelt's money raisers. He was appointed first chairman of the Securities and Exchange Commission, ironically outlawing the very stock manipulation tactics that he had used to build a fortune. And ultimately, in 1937, he was to be appointed ambassador of the United States to the Court of St. James's.

The time soon came when he was able to buy the sort of house he had dreamed of, a mansion, no less. He found it in a comfortable red brick house with many bathrooms, and he hired a decorator. What Rose Kennedy thought of rooms furnished in costly period furniture covered in fine silk, with delicate ornaments scattered about, I do not know. But it is evident that she wanted her house to be a home as well. For the children she bought child-sized chairs and for the furniture she had covers made of a serviceable material.

She was a balance to the daring, venturesome man who was the father of her children. To his impetuosity and competitiveness, she supplied calm reasonableness. To his demand of his sons that a Kennedy always win any race he chose to enter, she provided a counterdemand only that he do his best. Much as she loved her home, Rose Kennedy was far more than a homebody. She was herself, complete woman, whether in or out of the home. By 1938 she was a woman of the world, an ambassador's wife.

On a spring evening, husband and wife were dressing for dinner. "We've come a helluva long way from East Boston," Joseph Kennedy said. And Rose smiled lovingly, as though she had enjoyed every step of the way.

They were, in fact, in Windsor Castle, in a

suite once occupied by Queen Victoria, and they were to dine that evening with their majesties, King George and Queen Elizabeth. Joseph Kennedy had broken all records. He was an Irishman, a Roman Catholic, a second-generation immigrant, and he was the first of his kind to represent the United States. Yet he remained what he had always been, an uninhibited, brilliant, hardheaded, tempestuous character. He was accompanied by his beautiful, well-bred wife and surrounded by his lively swarming children. England loved them all, and Rose had more to do with that English acceptance than anyone knows.

The many escapades of the gay young Kennedys would not have been accepted, nor would the ambassador's refusal to wear the usual knee breeches and black silk stockings when presented at court but appeared instead in a full dress suit, had it not been for the conventionally beautiful woman at his side. Rose was not really conventional. She could and did act as independently as any woman when she chose, but she knew when to be conventional.

When she talked with the Queen, for example, as she did upon one occasion, at least, for more than half an hour, with her usual tact and instinctive understanding of another's personality she discussed with her royal hostess the womanly duties, common to both, of home and children, and to the Queen's query she revealed the fact that with a family of nine she was compelled to keep a chart of who had what childhood diseases and inoculations.

This instinctive understanding was never more active than in Rose Kennedy's relationship to the proud, sensitive, able man who was her husband. In public she never assumed leadership. But there were other times when he needed her strength and compassion and of these she gave with a whole and loving heart. For the man, so dominant, so self-confident, could upon occasion be desperately hurt.

A speech at a class luncheon at Harvard in praise of President Roosevelt was received without enthusiasm; his son Joe, a member of the scrub football team at Harvard for three years, was not given his chance to win his letter in his senior year; deepest wound of all, the ambassador never received an honorary degree from Harvard, his own alma mater, though other universities honored him —these wounds, seemingly slight for so successful a man, nevertheless cut deep and he refused any further financial help to Harvard, even to giving money to the Harvard Medical School for research into mental retardation.

At such times Rose stood steadfastly at his side, not questioning his right to decide, and supporting him with her unchanging faith in the man that he was. She gave him more than love. She gave such respect that she left him free to make his own decisions and abide by them, whatever the result.

Strength and compassion — these are the stuff of her nature, the essence of her womanhood.

The years in England were happy ones, in spite of the dark foreshadows of war to come. She, with husband and eight of her children, was a guest at the coronation of Pope Pius XII, and Ted, the youngest, received his first Holy Communion at that time.

Then Hitler declared war. Now Rose Kennedy had to face tragedy again as woman and mother. Her eldest son, Joe, was of an age for military service if the United States decided to join the European nations against Germany. All her heart was with her husband as he began his crusade against America's involvement.

Joseph Kennedy was bitterly attacked for his pacifist views. He continued to ignore his attackers in the Kennedy tradition. But he was falling from grace in the eyes of the New Deal.

In 1940 he was forced to retire from his post at the Court of St. James's, having made a firm statement that we should not support England, that our going to war to aid Britain would devastate America's resources.

His crusade for neutrality ended on December 7, 1941, when the Japanese bombed Pearl Harbor. In July Rose Kennedy's eldest son had joined the navy and become an aviation cadet.

3

A WOMAN never feels so lonely as she does during a war. It matters not that she is one of millions. She is alone. It is her own son whom she must now yield up to the possibility of death or mutilation, her son who is the fruit of her body, the child whom she has nurtured through all his growing years so that he may one day become a man.

Madame Kung was entirely correct in her estimate of her three sons. Of course they were the most important result of her life and work. She loved her daughters dearly but one son was more valuable than any number of daughters. Do not ask me why she felt it so. It is simply nature. The Chinese are not ashamed of basic human nature. They created their ancient system of law on basic human nature. Our Western system of law is corrective, not to say punitive of human nature. Chinese law is permissive of human nature. It takes into consideration human emotions.

When a woman gives birth to a daughter, Madame Kung used to say, she has only extended herself, she has merely produced more of the same. But when she gives birth to a son, she has outdone herself; she has created a new being, entirely different from herself. Through a son a woman reaches another world, the world of men. When she loses a son, she must retreat again into the shadowed world of women.

Rose Kennedy might, of course, deny that she shared this conception. We have never discussed it. Any strong, self-confident American woman might deny it, I suppose. Yet something of this original female feeling hides in all women, I observe, however it may be denied.

Now, true or not, Rose Kennedy had to face the possibility of death in her family, the death of her eldest son, a vigorous youthful copy of his father, and yet a young man of his own mind, who had made his independent decision to enter the war.

Then John, her second son, also voluntarily joined the navy. Now, there were two of them to pray for every day. She accepted the challenge of enduring what she had already learned with her retarded daughter, Rosemary. What could not be prevented or changed must be endured, and endured with calm resolution. She was prepared for tragedy.

It came in 1943. Her son John was missing in action. He had been skipper of a PT boat. The boat had been sunk under fire. The story has been told many times and I need not repeat it here. What is important to me is that for an entire month she did not know whether he was alive or dead. Her husband, always optimistic where his sons were concerned, believed that Jack would come out alive somehow and he refused to tell the news to his family. The parents waited, and prayed, and spent sleepless nights torn between hope and despair.

I have my own experience by which to judge. In that same war, I had a member of my family in the Battle of the Bulge. On Christmas Eve we had a telegram saying that he was missing in action. My house was full of children. Should they be told? No, they were too young to be robbed of Christmas joy. We who were their elders must conceal our anxiety, our fear, our rebellion. For three weeks we did not know whether life or death would be the next message. Fortunately for us, as for the Kennedys, it was life: life damaged, it is true, but life, in answer to prayer. For prayer is not only kneeling in a church. Prayer is the soul's intense desire. Prayer is longing crystallized in a word or two, or only longing which words cannot contain.

Rose Kennedy is fortunate in that she has faith

in a religion. The Roman Catholic faith especially, I think, provides the tools for prayer — the silence of a vast cathedral, the symbolism of lighted candles, the images of a kindly mother and her compassionate Savior son, the solemn rites performed by robed priests — all this induces faith, perhaps, or at least prescribes a path for the agonizing soul to follow. I am sure Rose Kennedy in the wisdom of her own experience followed the path in which her feet had been set from earliest childhood. Other women, lacking such a path, must find their own way to send their prayers to heaven.

Madame Kung had her own path. It was much like the one Rose Kennedy had. When the Japanese invaded China, and young Chinese men went to war to defend their country, her two eldest sons joined the Nationalist Army. While they were gone she went every day to the Buddhist temple in her city, and day and night two candles burned, one for each son, upon the altar before the huge golden Buddha. The priests in that temple, too, said Mass and she paid for them to do so. One day, however, she observed that one candle had burned more quickly than the other during the night and the straw wick had sunk into the tallow and had gone out. Instantly foreboding fell upon her. She lit a match and held it to the wick but it would not catch fire again.

"I knew a son was dead," she told me later.

It was her second son who fell in battle on that day. But Rose Kennedy was more fortunate. Her second son came home again, a hero. But a hero cursed to live the remaining days of his life in constant pain.

———•◆•◆•———

For a time it seemed that tragedy had been avoided for the Kennedy family. True, the husband and father was restless. There seemed to be no place at all for him now in the political scene as the war raged on. In 1940 he had been mentioned as a possible presidential candidate. Now, three years later, politicians avoided him.

There seemed nothing for him to do except to go on making money. This he did with his usual flair. Real estate, stocks, motion pictures, whatever he did made money. Rose Kennedy knew that the man she loved loved a power beyond the power of money. He wanted the power of government, and he would have it!

He began to dream for his sons. First he dreamed for his eldest, perhaps his dearest son, his namesake, his aide in leadership in the family, handsome, successful, brilliant Joe, Jr.

In 1943 young Joe went to England as a volunteer bomber pilot. According to a friend — I never met Joseph, Jr. — "He was the handsomest, the most brilliant of them all. And yet, I always felt he wanted to die. But people of courage and daring, people who are willing to take the risk of death, always want to die. They are always testing themselves, even to the ultimate.''

Young Joe was hopelessly in love with a beautiful Englishwoman. She, unfortunately, was already married. ''When hopelessness is the core of a man's being, he invites death every day,'' Joe's friend told me.

Joe fulfilled his mission in 1944 and was ordered home. He did not choose to go home. He decided to volunteer as pilot on a Liberator bomber to fly explosives toward the V-2 rocket sites the Germans had established in Normandy. The pilots would drop from the bomber by parachute over the channel near the coast of France, while the bomber would proceed under remote control to its target and crash.

Is it possible that this young man whose father's most ardent wish was that his son would, one day, be president of the United States, consciously or unconsciously, possessed an uncontrollable death wish?

With Joe was Lieutenant Wilford J. Willy, USN, of Fort Worth, Texas, also a volunteer, a man with a wife and three children. Tragedy fell again. On August 12, 1944, Lieutenant Joseph Kennedy and Lieutenant Wilford Willy were in their aircraft, accompanied by two Vega Venturas. Suddenly what had seemed a routine flight became disaster. Their plane exploded, cause unknown, and the two young men inside it were blown to bits. No trace was ever found of their bodies.

This was but a prelude to yet another, almost unbearable, tragedy. In the spring of 1943, Kathleen, the second eldest daughter, had gone to Europe as a Red Cross worker. With Rosemary away, Kathleen had assumed a special place in her family. The elder daughter at home is a special person. The mother looks to her for understanding and help. She helps the father to understand the mother. The father can see himself in boys. But his girls are enchantment, revelation.

Kathleen had the independent, forthright Kennedy temperament, and courage to do what she wanted to do. She was a leader among her sisters, as Joe was leader among his brothers, and this shared responsibility brought them close. There was a special bond between Joe and Kathleen.

When their father was ambassador to the Court of Saint James's, Kathleen, at eighteen, was sufficiently poised and self-assured to represent her mother at social functions and to be presented at court. Her parents were strict with her, however. She was not allowed to go to a nightclub, even though the invitation came from a Rockefeller. She was attractive to men. As one young man said, "Eunice is the most intelligent and Patricia is the prettiest of the girls, but Kathleen is the one you always remember."

While she was in England on a previous visit, before the war, she met William John Robert Cavendish, Marquess of Hartington and son of the Duke of Devonshire, scion of one of England's oldest and wealthiest families. A friendship developed between the two young people, who were still so young that it might be only an infatuation. They parted when the Kennedy family went back to the United States. In 1943, however, when Kathleen returned to England, the relationship deepened into love.

In 1944 she helped Billy Cavendish in a political campaign which he lost. By this time they knew they wanted to marry. The only obstacle was religion; he was Episcopalian, she was Catholic, and neither wanted to yield. Billy was willing to be married by a priest but would not agree that his children be raised as Roman Catholic. Kathleen would not be married with the Episcopalian service, for this meant excommunication from her own church. Since they could come to no agreement, they were married by a civil ceremony.

Rose at that time was ill in a hospital. She heard of the marriage from a nurse and was prepared by foreknowledge against the press, waiting outside her door. She would not speak to the newspapermen, for she would not judge her young people. The problem was theirs, she said.

She knew, of course, that the civil marriage was no marriage at all in the eyes of her church, and that her daughter, forbidden to take the sacraments, would at Easter be excommunicated. But still she did not interfere. Her self-discipline controlled her. Moreover, she understood that the same self-discipline was manifest in Kathleen. Like mother, like daughter?

In any event, by the time the fateful Easter came, Kathleen, now the Marchioness of Hartington, was already a widow. When her brother Joe was killed, she flew back to the United States to be with her parents. While she was there, she received word that young Billy Cavendish, her husband, had also been killed in action. They had been together only a few weeks before he was called to France with his regiment, the Coldstream Guards. He was killed in infantry action in Normandy. As son and heir of the Duke of Devonshire, the Marquess would have succeeded to his father's title. Kathleen would have become first lady-in-waiting to Queen Elizabeth and Mistress of the Royal Robes.

Upon the news of his death, the British government sent a plane for Kathleen and immediately after the funeral she went into retreat and was reconciled with her church. "God has taken care of the problem in His own way," she wrote to a friend.

And Billy's mother, the Duchess of Devonshire, wrote to Rose Kennedy, "I want to tell you of the joy that Kathleen brought into my son's life." They had been married four months.

For some years after her husband's death, Kathleen lived on in England, busying herself mainly with charity work. She missed her family, and yet she was not ready to leave the land of the man she had loved so much. Then one day in May,

1948, she heard that her father was in Paris on his way to the Riviera. She decided to fly to France and be with him. A friend, Earl Fitzwilliam, was flying in his own plane to Cannes to inspect a stable of racehorses.

"Why not come along with me?" he asked. She agreed and they crossed the channel safely. When they reached France, however, it was night and dark and foggy. Near the little town of Privas, it grew difficult to see and their plane crashed into a mountain.

Both Kathleen and Fitzwilliam were instantly killed. Did Kathleen, too, have a death wish? At a certain point one does not think of danger because it no longer matters. When life has too little value, then the chance of death holds little fear.

When Kathleen was found, she lay as though she were sleeping, only a small cut on her head and one shoe slipped off. The villagers carried her body down the mountain to Privas and her heartbroken father came and took her to England. She was buried beside her husband, Billy Cavendish. Thus ended, in total tragedy, the story of the second daughter of the Kennedy family.

———

There was no exact counterpart in the Kung family on the other side of the world, and yet that family had a daughter, too, who experienced love and death. Mei-lan, or Beautiful Orchid, was her name. The Kung family was modern for its time and when Mei-lan had insisted on a university education, she had been allowed to attend the University of Peking. Then she fell in love with a brilliant young man. Religion did not keep them apart, but family tradition did.

Each of them had been betrothed in childhood to persons belonging to great old families, and each family insisted that the engagement be honored. Mei-lan was compelled to marry a man she did not love. She went through the ceremony bravely. I was a guest at the wedding, and I saw her, pale and beautiful, in her pink brocaded satin wedding gown. She behaved with the dignity befitting the elder daughter of a great Chinese family, but there was no light in her eyes.

She went through the three-day ceremony with unchanging grace. On the fourth day I was wakened early in the morning by a message to come at once to the Kung household. I went and found the family in frightful grief. Mei-lan had been brought home dead. She had hanged herself in the night. Rising from her marriage bed, she had gone to an empty room and, taking the wide silk sash from her nightdress, she had tied one end of it to a beam and the other end about her neck. When she was discovered, her body was cold. On the same night, in the same city, her lover had shot himself. Obviously it was a death pact.

Joseph Patrick Kennedy went home alone. He sailed back and on the voyage seldom left his stateroom and seldom spoke to anyone. To reporters when he arrived, he shrugged his shoulders. "Nothing means anything anymore," he said. "There's nothing I can say."

His daughter, Patricia, met him at the dock. They kissed in silence and walked silently to the long black car. Rose, the mother, was waiting at home, and it was to her he went.

I wonder if I have overemphasized the quality of gentleness in Rose Kennedy. Have I confused gentleness with the ability to accept? And whence comes this ability to accept the inevitable? I believe Rose Kennedy believes in the existence of God; of a wise, all-knowing, all-planning God. After the most recent tragedy to come upon the family, the tragedy that has fallen upon the youngest son, Senator Edward M. Kennedy, Rose Kennedy, who is approaching her eightieth year of life, declared, "This is a good life. God does not send us a cross any heavier than we can bear. . . . How you cope is the important thing, not the events themselves. . . . I am sure Ted can rise above all this."

A few days after Kathleen's funeral, Rose returned to her usual program of life: at seven in the morning Mass at St. Francis Xavier Church in Hyannis, breakfast with her husband, a noontime swim in her pool or in Nantucket Sound, an afternoon of golf, her heavy correspondence, her work for the mentally retarded, her reading, her hours with her husband.

Under her quiet reserve there is something not at all gentle, something fiercely determined, something totally controlled, something ironhard. She has learned to cope.

When I went to visit Madame Kung after Meilan's death, I found her not at home. Her bondmaid said she was at the Buddhist temple, praying for her daughter's soul. I went there and, directed by a gray-robed priest, I found her in the alcove of the goddess of mercy. She stood before the goddess with bowed head, telling her beads, and murmuring the Buddhist ritual prayer:

O mi t'o fu — o mi t'o fu —

I did not disturb her. For I saw that she, too, was learning to cope.

*T*HE Kennedy clan closed in and moved to the next son, John Fitzgerald Kennedy.

Did the next son, after his brother's death, really want to take his place in the race for the presidency? Personally, I doubt it. He was already a published writer. He was beginning to be a good political thinker, as well as a writer. He was coming out of the jungle of life so inevitable to a large family. The Kennedy "jungle" was so dense, so close, that Eunice Shriver once said it was remarkable that any of them ever married, they were so busy with one another's activities.

Joseph Patrick himself told an interviewer, "I put Jack into politics; I was the one. I told him Joe was dead and therefore it was his responsibility to run for politics. He didn't want to. He felt he didn't have the ability and he still feels that way. But I told him he had to."

I wonder whether Jack Kennedy ever dreamed of another life, a quieter life, with books and friends and family, perhaps, and of living long and growing old. Death is sad only when it comes to the young. And what of his young wife, Jacqueline? Would she have been happier as a woman than she is now, the wife of one of the world's richest men, and a man so much older than herself?

The second son's ascension was rapid. He was mentioned for governor of Massachusetts. But this was not direct enough for the father. He decided Jack's path to the White House lay through the Senate. He was already a congressman. To become a senator, he must displace Henry Cabot Lodge, Jr.

He began at once to make himself well known throughout the state, appearing everywhere. Through the next three years he was indomitable. Behind him stood his indomitable family. It is a proof of greatness when out of tragedy new enterprise is undertaken.

The symbolism of the phoenix, rising from ashes but created by distinctive fire, becomes more profound as one ponders it. A truly great family defies the tragedies that befall it. The blow falls, it is received, it is absorbed, it is defied, it is transmuted into new energy. Lesser folk cannot achieve the transmutation because they cannot muster the energy. Defiance is based on anger, and only the strong can be angry enough to defy even the gods. The Kennedys are strong enough to accept, strong enough to be angry, strong enough to use their anger to create another step toward their unchanging goal, the achievement of power.

As I study the individuals of this amazing family, I see that power has always been unquestionably the constant goal. It is not for the sake of what power can accomplish. The Kennedy men honestly believed that they were not self-seeking, that they were capable of using their power only for good, and, therefore, that they had a moral obligation to seek for and assume power. The father of the family believed in this philosophy and taught it to his sons. He was practical enough to know, however, that in the United States money is the basis for power. Therefore, he devoted himself to making money. He taught his sons the uses of money. He worked to give them money as the tool for power. Guns serve in nondemocratic countries, and by use of arms dictators are made. But in democracies money is the essential for power.

When John F. Kennedy moved into place there was plenty of money in the Kennedy family: millions of dollars and millions more to come. Joseph P. Kennedy was perhaps one of the wealthiest self-made men in the world.

Once the plan for John's achieving power was set, the whole family rallied behind it. Though a pro-Eisenhower movement was rising in the country, John Kennedy announced that he was a candidate from Massachusetts for the Senate.

"When you have beaten Lodge, you will have the best," his father said. "Why try for something less?"

It was an echo of the old battle cry, "If you play at all, play to win and win at the top."

The whole family responded to the cry. The women, as always, followed their men without reservation. There were "Kennedy teas" and "Coffee with the Kennedys," and Kennedy daughters going from house to house, fresh young girls, pleasant to look at, with the confident good humor characteristic of a family sure of its own position.

Even the mother, Rose Kennedy, joined the campaign, and it was as a mother, as well as the wife of an ambassador and the daughter of a former political favorite of Boston, that she visited the Italian wives and mothers and was able to speak with them in Italian. In short, the Kennedys were everywhere, to the discomfort of the opposition.

"Holy hell, every place you look there's a Kennedy," a man lamented.

Two other aspects of the campaign impress me, however, even more than the fact of its success. First, it showed the recuperative powers of a well-founded family. Individually and together they could not be defeated. When one member is killed, the others come closer together than before and immediately the set goal is pursued more hotly than before.

Second, the secret strength of such families is

in their ability to unite into a single driving force for achievement. Of course so large a family has its divisions, its secret quarrels, its private prejudices, its individual preferences. But the world does not know them. The great family is always a closed corporation. Together they stand and will stand. Though only two members may remain someday, they will still stand side by side. This quality of loyalty, too, is a secret of a great family's power, and the Kennedys have the secret. If it can be passed on to the new generation, the Kennedy family will be a power in our nation for a long time to come.

So far as the world can see, the women in this competitive family remain unshakably behind their men. They are units in the whole. Individualistic, strong, sometimes arbitrary, they are sure of themselves as women and as members of the family. Each adds her own talent to the family scene, but it is always within the background of the family.

The least allied perhaps was Jacqueline Bouvier. We do not know what might have become of that marriage if John Kennedy had not become president of the United States. Rumor is not to be trusted nor indeed does it matter, for all private possibilities were put aside when the larger good of the family was concerned.

When sons married, their wives became part of the Kennedy family, just as in old China the daughters-in-law became members of the Kung family. Both families accepted the new members as a matter of course.

In 1950 Robert Kennedy, "Bobby" as the family and most of the world knew him, married Ethel Skakel, and in 1953 Jack Kennedy, now in the position of eldest son and leader of the younger generation, married Jacqueline Bouvier.

Jacqueline had more than beauty. She had a strong will and answered her father-in-law's occasional fits of temper with her own flashing determination. Fortunately the aging old eagle liked a fiery woman, and after a shocked instant he could laugh.

The 1950s were the years of political division in China, not of unity. I do not know what might have happened had not the catastrophe of revolution destroyed the structure of the ancient government and set up instead two revolutionary governments, the first Nationalist, the second Communist.

One of the sons of the Kung family joined the Nationalists, another son the Communists, and thereafter the family divided into two parts, passing from mutual disapproval and anger to active hatred. It was the beginning of the end of their greatness. Even the father, Mr. Kung, was helpless in the surge of new times.

There was no division in the Kennedy family, there was complete loyalty among its members. The parents were the center from which the loyalty radiated, but the members, encouraged by family approval, were able to function upon their own invention and strength. Thus Jack Kennedy, supported wholeheartedly, developed the ability to think his own thoughts, define his own plans, direct his own fortunes.

It was he who made the final decision to run for the presidency and, though he consulted with his father, it was no more than seeking advice which he might or might not follow.

The father was wise enough to understand his own success. His son was now a man. He withdrew from the scene, keeping in touch, but from a distance. When his son was elected, he absented himself from the first triumphant moment, but the young President-elect, missing him, went back into the family home and together they returned to greet the press, father and son. Joseph Kennedy wanted the world to know that now his son was entirely his own master. There would be no behind-the-scenes in the White House.

This resolute withdrawal, so fortunate for all concerned, was the consequence of an honest faith in his children. As for John's choice of Bobby as attorney general, the father said:

"Jack's lucky to have Bobby in that job. He'll make a hell of a good attorney general. After all, very few attorney generals of the past have had the court experience Bobby has. And very few have his ability as an organizer."

He scoffed at the accusation of nepotism. Why should a son of his need a job? And though he and the mother went to Washington for the inauguration, they announced that they would not live there or anywhere near. And they kept their word.

Inexorable tragedy, however, which always befell the Kennedy family after a high success, struck again. The father was at the height of his personal success and triumph. At a moment when he seemed in full health, he suffered a stroke.

It was the Christmas season, 1961, the family was gathering at the huge Palm Beach estate. The day was so fine that Joseph Kennedy decided to play golf. After the sixth hole he suddenly did not feel well and he called for his car and went home. Once there, he refused to have a doctor called and was on his way to his room to rest when suddenly he collapsed.

At the hospital the stroke was pronounced to be slight, but it was enough to cripple his right side and, greatest change of all, to silence the strong loud voice which in anger or command could roar through the house. The entire family hastened to his bedside and joined in prayer. Cardinal Cushing came in to bless him.

On the day before Christmas a tracheotomy was performed to help him breathe. A week later he began to improve, but he was never the same again. In effect, John Fitzgerald Kennedy, the new president of the United States, became the practical, if not the titular, head of the Kennedy family.

*I*T IS now that a new figure takes precedence among the Kennedy women. Jacqueline Bouvier Kennedy took her place not only as the President's wife and First Lady, but as a Kennedy, and the mother of Kennedy children.

Who was she, who is she, in her own right? Let me tell first of the sight of her. I first met her at the dinner the President and Mrs. Kennedy gave for the Nobel Prize winners of the nation. It was the first time we had been so honored, heretofore our presidents seemingly embarrassed by our company. But President Kennedy and his lady were not uneasy in the presence of intellectuals and we all waited in the East Room for their arrival.

I had met enough officials in the world so that I was not unduly moved by the prospect of meeting another president in my own country, although I am always properly patriotic, I hope. But I confess to a stir in my heart, a surge of pride, when to the tune of martial music our young President and his wife were announced. We Nobel Prize winners, all except I scientists, stood in a waiting line.

The music rose and then came a flutter of colorful flags, carried by an honor guard of strong, dashing young men, and behind them, side by side, appeared our handsome young President and his graceful wife. Both were smiling, both were stunningly good to look at, both were in gay spirits and the very picture of health, youth, and beauty. They looked the way rulers should look, whatever their titles might be, prince and princess, king and queen, maharajah and maharanee, president and wife.

The guests were for the moment only spectators and burst into applause. One felt a wave of love and admiration flow out from us toward the spectacular couple who, smiling and unaffected, came toward us to shake hands with us in welcome. We are not accustomed to such recognition and appreciation, and I saw tears in the eyes of some of the older men.

Jacqueline looked so regal, yet shy, and her voice, which I had heard previously only on television, was even more low and soft. Yet my female instincts told me there was unyielding firmness beneath that fragile facade.

Later, I had full opportunity to observe Jacqueline Kennedy, for I sat at her small table. During the Kennedy regime it was customary to seat guests at small round tables rather than at a long table. The occasion of the dinner for Nobel Prize winners was dedicated especially to General George Marshall and Ernest Hemingway, both of whom were dead. Their widows had the seats of honor at the President's table.

I was fortunate enough to sit beside the astronaut, John Glenn, whom I had very much wanted to meet, and I fear my dinner conversation was mainly with him, rather than with my hostess. But I observed her, of course, as one woman will watch another, especially one lovely as she, and I observed her many changes of mood. Expressions of concern and merriment and chagrin drifted across her face as her conversation changed. She responded differently to each one who spoke to her.

I do not mean that to sound cruel or denigrating. I doubt not for a moment that she was sincere in her reactions, but her reactions are swift. She is, of course, an enigma, and totally unpredictable. Presidential aide David Powers summed it up quite neatly, "Just when you are sure you know her, be careful."

Eleanor Roosevelt once said, "There is a great deal more to her than meets the eye," and *that* First Lady was a keen judge of human nature. Actually, Jacqueline was, undoubtedly, the most talked about and admired president's wife since Eleanor herself.

Like Eleanor, she did as she pleased. She was, critics moaned, too independent, too superior to be a "good wife" for a president. She was not the "typical American" — whatever that may be.

Was she not "good wife" material because she had been taught to ride and loved it and did not intend to give it up? Or was it because she knew good furniture and abhorred bad taste? She made many changes in the White House. She tried to make it the kind of residence it should be. And to my mind, she succeeded more than any of her predecessors.

"Before Jackie," a society columnist wrote, "the White House looked like a Statler Hotel, even the ashtrays seemed straight out of the Army PX!"

Soon the so-called common man began to accept her, not for what she did but, rather, the manner in which she did it.

Her I'll-do-it-my-way attitude was truly American. And if she spoke foreign languages and wrote poems and read French novels and enjoyed the ballet, well, she also went through the dusty White House storerooms and shoved furniture aside, pulled out long-forgotten and neglected American treasures and had them restored and placed where visitors, too, could see them and, seeing them, recall our heritage and be proud.

Oddly enough, she captured all ages and both genders, if she appealed to them at all. Young girls copied her hairstyles, her simple, sleeveless dresses, her short, immaculate white gloves, and even her breathless, little-girl speech.

Others were impressed by her poise, her femininity, her obvious love for Caroline and John. The public never tired of reading about her and her beautiful children, no matter how trivial the event. She became a Super Star, an Idol. And as I observed her at dinner that night, I learned why: She seemed to be the perfect wife, mother, sweetheart, indeed, the perfect woman.

After dinner we were all directed back to the East Room again, where proper, straight-backed, gilded chairs had been set up in rows, ready for the evening's entertainment. Strange the moments that remain in one's memory! I remember that while we were waiting for the President and Mrs. Kennedy to rejoin us, one of the two honor guests, a kindly elderly lady, came to me and said, "I enjoyed your book *So Big*."

Not wanting to embarrass her by telling her that I had not written that book, I merely smiled and thanked her. Fortunately, the President had returned, and it was he who interrupted with a sudden question to me.

"What do you think we should do about Korea?" he asked.

I had recently been to Korea, but at this moment that troubled country was far from my thoughts.

"Why do you ask, Mr. President?" I countered.

"Because we can't go on as we are," he replied in his quick, direct fashion. "Japan must help us to rebuild."

I knew very well the feelings of the Koreans toward the Japanese, the result of centuries of history, but there was no time to begin on that, especially as dear old Robert Frost, always jealous of the President's attention, now interrupted us.

"Mr. President," I said, "I am writing an historical novel about Korea now which explains the present situation in terms of the past. It is called *The Living Reed.* I'll send you the first copy."

Alas, when the first book came off the press and I sent it to him, he was in Texas, and before he could come home again to the White House, he was dead. My fondest memory of him and his attractive wife is that night when both were at the height of their youth and vitality.

The entertainment of the remainder of the evening precluded my having prolonged or serious conversation with Mrs. Kennedy. My first discovery was her shyness. It had not been apparent to me before, although it should have been. I, too, am shy. — painfully so. Even to this day I dread meeting strangers. There is always an apprehension. I want to flee. And I felt this in Jacqueline, too. In my brief exchanges with her, I found her withdrawn, as though she were not altogether among us, nor wanted to be: a quality natural to her, I was to discover, and easily understood when one knows her family history.

Later, in India, when my own visit followed immediately after hers, everyone, it seemed, questioned me about her and wanted to share with me their impressions of her.

Of course, I was eager to know what the people thought of her. It was expected that, in her inexperience there, she occasionally violated Indian customs. But question as I did, I heard no lack of respect. The most critical remark, if one can call it such, came from an intimate friend of mine, a woman high in government.

"She is like a young girl just out of finishing school. But she is trying very hard to do everything nicely and to be very good, because she is the wife of your President."

It seemed a simple remark and yet there was truth in it. Jacqueline Onassis is not a Kennedy. She is not a leader by birth and tradition as the Kennedys are. There have been charming, well-bred, delightful people in the Bouvier family, but no leaders and very little family tradition. She has nothing to convey to a new generation. Her children will absorb from her the good taste, the artistic tendencies, the love of beauty so natural to her. But it is doubtful if they will become leaders in the sense that Ethel Kennedy's children may.

I found that people in India, too, felt the quality of aloneness in her. The Indians are a supersensitive people, their natural intelligence reaching almost to the point of clairvoyance, and they understood amazingly well the complex troubled, beauty-loving nature of Jacqueline Kennedy.

"She will always be unhappy somewhere in her being," a wise and old man told me. "She is made up of sunshine and shadow, as time is made up of day and night."

Let me proceed to my own analysis of this admired and disliked woman, so beautiful and in her own way so strong and so lonely.

She, too, came of a great family, one whose history in some ways resembles that of the Kennedys though the Kennedys were from Ireland and the Bouviers from the south of France. The Bouvier ancestor who came to the United States was a simple young man of twenty-three, an infantryman in the army of the defeated Napoleon, and an apprentice cabinetmaker by trade from Pont-Saint-Esprit, a small village on the Rhone in historic Languedoc about seventy miles from the Mediterranean coast.

Men of Ireland are warmhearted and tempestuous, and so are the men of the Mediterranean. Michel Bouvier was as impulsive and adventuresome as Patrick Joseph Kennedy was when he emigrated to the new country. Even the time was in the same half of a century, the Irishman in 1849, the Frenchman in 1815.

If I lay emphasis on family, it is because I have come to believe, in the process of my ever lengthening life, that what we are is far more the result of ancestry than of environment and Jacqueline Bouvier is strongly the result of her ancestry. She has qualities like and unlike those of Jack Kennedy. They shared the American tradition of a family of humble beginnings rising quickly into near aristocracy. They were both intellectuals not by inheritance but by acquired tastes. Neither had the profound grounding in and natural instinct for intellectualism to be found in families where generations have been intellectuals.

Both Kennedys and Bouviers share the original earthiness that comes from earthy origins and perhaps too swift success. Both families are based on a stout, strong single ancestor, Patrick Joseph Kennedy and Michel Bouvier. But there is an essential difference between the families.

The Kennedys today are still a great family. The Bouviers are so no longer. The Kennedys still stand together as a unit, men, women, and children; the Bouviers are divided into a dissident handful of persons who live separate lives. Loyalty and mutual approval continue to be the secret of Kennedy strength. Even in the recent rumors of scandal surrounding Ted and the late Mary Jo Kopechne, there was no sign of family dissidence or evidence of loss of confidence in him. They are still positive that they can cope. I again explain this unifying strength only by believing that it comes from their common goal, the achievement of political power.

Jacqueline Kennedy had a strong first American ancestor in Michel Bouvier, the carpenter. He moved to Philadelphia, where many French had settled. Two other Frenchmen helped to establish him in business, Joseph Bonaparte, the exiled King of Spain, and Stephen Girard. Both were wealthy and loved fine furniture.

In the summer of 1816 Michel did some work for the ex-king at his summer place, Point Breeze, a mansion near Bordentown on the Jersey side of the Delaware River, set in a landscape of ten farms. From being a carpenter Michel Bouvier advanced to being a cabinetmaker.

In 1818 he went to work for Joseph Bonaparte and did so well that the next year he opened his own shop. Point Breeze burned down two years later and he was asked to superintend the rebuilding. For three years he did superintend the entire project, maintaining at the same time his own fine furniture shop in Philadelphia.

After some years of increasing prosperity, in June, 1822, Michel married Sarah Anne Pearson. Two years passed and a son was born, whom Michel named Eustache, and so the Bouviers were established as an American family. True, their success financially was still modest, and socially they were still working people. Nevertheless Michel was a dreamer as well as a worker and he could look ahead into unlimited heights in the new country. Ten years had passed since he had stepped on these shores, and in another ten years what might not happen?

A second child, a daughter, was born to him, and all looked bright ahead. But success again invited tragedy. When the baby girl was only five months old, Sarah, his young wife, died. He was crushed, he was discouraged, but it was too late to go home to France. All his investment was now in the United States. He could do nothing but work harder at his trade.

Michel Bouvier eventually married again. His second wife's name was Louise Vernou, and from this strong woman he had ten children besides every imaginable other benefit. She was enterprising, vital, ambitious, and of blue blood. Her family was not rich, but her father was a French nobleman and her grandfather was one of Washington's officers. Moreover, she was well educated. All this Michel lacked.

Success seemed now to be the pattern of his life. By the time he reached fifty, he was a prosperous importer and manufacturer. His wife was thirty years old. They had seven daughters and a seventeen-year-old son from Michel's two marriages. Eustache was a charming and handsome boy and, although he was spoiled by his stepmother and many sisters, Michel expected much from him. The stern, demanding father, without knowing it, kept the son a perpetual child.

In the thirty years remaining in his life, Michel

acquired more real estate, made more money, and sired four more children, including sons named John Vernou and Michel Charles. Now the founder of the family was content.

In 1853 he sold his coal and timber lands in West Virginia at profits so enormous that Philadelphia society forgot his humble origin and welcomed him into their sacred company. He built a huge mansion, and took his large family on a European tour, making a triumphal visit to his native village of Pont-Saint-Esprit, where he was received as a returning monarch.

Great joy came with the birth of their first grandson, born in 1865 to John Vernou and his wife Carrie. In 1873, however, a depression fell on Philadelphia and, indeed, on the nation. It was more than a financial depression for Michel, then eighty-one years of age, for the year before he had lost his wife and, without her, his loneliness was insupportable.

By June, 1874, it was evident that his active, successful life was coming to an end. He had made a complicated, careful will, protecting especially his daughters. He died at the age of eighty-two.

After his death, his two younger sons, John Vernou and Michel Charles, centered their interests in Wall Street. The Bouvier family still seemed to remain close, though divided geographically between New York and Philadelphia. The second generation of Bouviers displayed such luxury it seemed beyond imagination that, in so short a space of time, money enough could have been made and spent.

Michel Charles lived in a palatial home in New York with his three sisters, Zénaïde, Alexine, and Mary. All were unmarried and remained so. The Bouviers had money enough by the time they reached the second generation to have influenced the country, but instead they used their fortune to establish an aristocratic image of themselves.

This feat was finally accomplished during the eighteen nineties when John Vernou Bouvier, Jr., found a noble family in France named Bouvier de la Fontaine and appropriated them as ancestors. He took their coat of arms and its motto and endeavored also to establish their connection with the family of Vernoho de Bonneuil. Whether these ancestors were authentic scarcely matters. The interesting fact is that they seemed to give comfort to the Bouvier family in the United States, and the security they had lacked.

Thereafter Michel Charles Bouvier devoted himself to using his money in the way he considered suitable to a man of high lineage. He loved fine living, and was devoted to his nephew, John Vernou Bouvier, Jr. The boy's father, John Vernou, Sr., had remained a stockbroker and had failed to amass the vast wealth of his brother, Michel. From his father's quiet household, John, Jr., would go to the opulent, formal home of his uncle where his spinster aunts would spoil and adore him, and where he learned to enjoy good living and style.

He grew into a tall, handsome man, a Major Judge Advocate in World War I. He was self-confident enough by that time, for he had heard all his life the constant refrain: The family depended upon him alone, he was their only hope, for without him the family would become extinct.

He realized his responsibilities, for all the love had not spoiled him. He was the first Bouvier to receive a college education and was graduated from Columbia University in 1882, a Phi Beta Kappa and class valedictorian. For his profession, he decided on law.

At the age of twenty-four he married Maude Sergeants, a beautiful young Englishwoman whose father was a prosperous manufacturer. The beauty of later Bouviers would be inherited mostly from her.

John and Maude first had a son and then another son and then a daughter. For ten years there were no more children and then, unexpectedly, twin girls were born, children fair and red haired, totally different from the others. Maude and Michelle developed into helpful industrious girls, of great help to their aging parents and a mainstay in the family.

John Bouvier III, their firstborn, became a handsome, charming, restless young man and the father of Jacqueline Bouvier Kennedy.

I can imagine the effect, the influence, of a father like Jack Bouvier on a sensitive, always lovely little girl. There were two little girls, Jacqueline and Lee, but Lee depended upon the older sister. Jacqueline was the leader, but I doubt that she enjoyed the position. Naturally shy, naturally withdrawn, naturally proud, naturally and perhaps abnormally perceptive of the opinions of other people, she had perforce to learn to be self-sufficient and in self-sufficiency find the base for such security as her life could offer.

It was not much. Her father was a true Bouvier in many ways. He had gone to Yale, had graduated in 1914 without significance, had found a job in a Wall Street brokerage firm through the help of a brother-in-law, and, with his quick mind and charming manners, he had done well. Then came World War I.

With his upbringing he did not relish the idea of military service, but he joined the navy and then, with help, transferred to the army where he found life more tolerable. He became engaged, then broke the engagement, a pattern that was to continue during the years. He went through the war, was honorably discharged in the spring of 1919, returned to his job on Wall Street where he was given a seat on the exchange. With financial aid from an adoring aunt, he planned soon to be very rich.

In the meantime he rented a fine apartment on Park Avenue and gave stupendous parties, and enjoyed attractive women and pretty girls. His striking good looks, his equally striking tailor-made clothes, his dashing sense of style made him a fascinating character. His French ancestry rather than the British accounted for his dark complexion, which he made darker by tan. So dark indeed was he that he was called "Black Jack," or "the Black Prince." He was dramatic and self-absorbed, in company preferring to create and stay in the limelight rather than take the trouble to learn to know other people. This, of course, made him always basically lonely, although he was sought after and spectacular in New York society. Of course money, much money, was necessary in order for him to live with the style in which he was determined to live.

The United States was going through all the license, all the daring freedoms, all the experimentation of the twenties. The effects were serious on various members of the Bouvier family, but Jack showed no signs of failure. He was a notable success on Wall Street and, to the delight of his family, he wanted to settle down and marry. To the surprise of New York society, however, he did not marry one of the obvious possibilities. Instead he chose Janet Lee, a girl much younger than himself and a friend of his twin sisters.

Everyone thought this engagement would be broken as others had been, but they did not know Janet Lee. She was of stronger character than most, and had every intention, amounting indeed to determination, of marrying Jack Bouvier.

She was the second generation of an Irish family new to wealth. Her father was the man who had brought the family in one generation to wealth and social success, not to mention the siring of three beautiful daughters. But the Bouviers, with much the same background, were two generations ahead in wealth and aristocracy and Janet clung to her Jack, in spite of prevailing doubts. They made a strikingly handsome couple, he so dark, she so fair.

Life seemed bright as sunshine ahead of the young pair. Money kept rolling in, and on July 28, 1929, Jack and Janet became the parents of an eight-pound daughter, whom they named Jacqueline, after the father.

Tragedy followed the joy of Jacqueline's birth. Jack's brother, Bud, died, a hopeless alcoholic. Six days after the funeral, panic fell on Wall Street and eight days after that a gigantic sell-off led to the greatest depression the United States had ever known, a depression that affected the world.

The Bouviers had been at the height of their financial success. Huge profits piled up and only a few persons, none of them Bouviers, were wise enough to be seriously alarmed. True, old Michel Charles had been the most prudent. When the panic was over, although more than half his fortune was gone, he still had enough to live on in reasonable comfort.

For Jack Bouvier the future was dark indeed.

So severe were his losses that he never recovered. He was compelled to ask help from his family, a situation humiliating enough for a proud luxury-loving man, but his family was unable to provide him with substantial help, and he was obliged to humble himself and ask aid from his father-in-law, James Lee, with whom he had never been friendly.

Lee was a solid character, a self-made millionaire before he was thirty. He agreed to help Jacqueline's father only if Jack would give up his expensive habits and his fashionable way of living. In the end Jack and his family moved, rent free, into an apartment owned by Lee, and from then on James Lee controlled expenditure. It was a swift fall in one short year.

In the summer of 1931 Jack and his family rented a cottage in East Hampton, near the rest of the Bouviers. And that summer little Jacqueline was in the society columns as having appeared with her parents at a dog show and as having had a party to celebrate her second birthday. Her father still suffered from the depression, as did all the Bouviers, but most of them were unable to change their way of living and dipped into capital. Even Jack still kept a stable of horses.

All the Bouviers believed that the depression would not last. But it did, and as year dragged into year they found themselves sinking back into the dreary middle class from which they had escaped a generation before.

In 1935 Michel Charles died, leaving his fortune well distributed among his family. Jack's cash amount was small but he had inherited his grandfather's business, and from it formed a new stock brokerage firm, which did well in its first years.

Tragedy waited, however. As his business prospered, his marriage began to fail. The trying years had been too much, apparently, for Jack Bouvier and Janet Lee Bouvier. Instead of coming closer first in adversity and then in new prosperity, they drew further apart. Wife and children stayed on in the apartment and Jack moved to a hotel room. Even the children could not keep them together.

For Jack Bouvier the loss of his daughters was heartbreaking. He loved them extravagantly, and showed it. He liked to have them with him, he liked to show them off, to teach them to ride, to laugh and play and joke with them. Jealous of the Lee family, he indulged the little girls in the hope of winning their love for him above all others. He kept three horses for them, he let them have a charge account in his name at a department store and gave them monthly allowances — small, to be sure, but more than he could afford. And he took them often to see the Bouvier relatives, to offset the Lees.

Between the two, the little girls grew up with divided hearts, but, during those years, their first love went to their father. He was exciting, gay, generous, fun to be with in contrast to the somewhat colorless, conventional mother. His influence prevailed during these important growing years.

———•—•—•—•———

I do not doubt, for example, that Jacqueline Kennedy's love of beauty, her sense of drama and style, came from her father. He was careful about his own appearance and he pointed out to her what he liked or disliked in the appearance of women they saw. He taught her how to wear clothes with distinction, as he himself did. So the girls learned that, though they might wear clothes not different from those of other girls, there must always be the illusion of difference.

And he taught his daughters that this difference must be expressed not only in clothes. It must be expressed even more explicitly in behavior. A woman, he taught them, must be a mystery. She must be withdrawn, reserved, slow to yield to a man's advances. As he pursued, she must retreat, she must withhold, she must charm by her silence, by her reticence rather than by her revelations. She must be the antithesis of aggressiveness, of masculinity.

Jack Bouvier had his daughters to himself in the summers and so there was plenty of time to impress his lessons upon them. The daughters went about their own employments, seeming to need no other company than their own. When they did appear at a family function, it was an event. The girls saw for themselves the validity of their father's principles. And Jacqueline, who admired her father and loved him above all others, learned his lessons well.

As Jacqueline developed into her teens, he praised her to her face, in the presence of others, openly and frequently. She was the prettiest girl in the world. If she was all this now, what would she be at twenty? She was the best equestrienne in the world already. If a cousin teased her or troubled her, Jack threatened the most violent punishment. Of course, Jacqueline blossomed under the father's praise and protection. She learned to admire herself in the shelter of his adulation and protection.

So it might have continued forever had not her mother married again, or had she married a lesser person than Hugh Auchincloss, a man of vast fortune and great respectability.

The Auchincloss family was a notable one. Brilliant marriages, great business acumen, solid Presbyterian virtues had found their culmination after generations in the person of Hugh Auchincloss. He was not at all like Jack Bouvier. Tall, heavy-boned, ruddy in complexion, he gave the impression of total honesty and stability, he inspired and deserved confidence, and he welcomed Janet Bouvier's pretty daughters into his family, and into his handsome homes, winter at Merrywood and summer at Hammersmith Farm.

Now Jacqueline had three families and it

became increasingly difficult for Jack Bouvier to maintain his hold on his daughters. He was a very different man when he had to attend Bouvier birthday and Christmas parties without them. There was nothing to talk about and no one to show off. He grew more and more indignant as time went on, for though he continued to support his daughters, to pay for their education and keep up their charge accounts at various department stores, he saw less and less of them. Yet he never gave up hope of winning them back, for he could not believe they enjoyed the staid Auchincloss environment. His daughters? No! They would come back to him. Surely they would come back to him once they were bored with the new scene.

What Jack Bouvier did not understand, perhaps, was that in demanding his daughters' preference and love, he was dividing them and building into their lives a deep incurable sense of insecurity. Where did they really belong? And which were the people who loved them most? These were the questions and there were no answers. There would never be any answers.

The degeneration of Jack Bouvier was hastened by the growing animosity of his father, John Vernou, Jr. Jack was now fifty, and he showed no more growth in the qualities of leadership than he had shown at twenty. Was he to be the perpetual playboy?

The family would have no head when he, John Vernou Bouvier, Jr., died. This Bouvier generation, so far as his sons were concerned, was a failure. He could only look to his grandsons. His pessimism was deepened by his worsening health until in 1948 he died. Jack headed the funeral procession. He was now the head of the Bouvier family.

He was the head of the family, and yet he could not keep them together. They did not respect him. In their opinion he had made no achievement worthy of respect. They did not heed his advice. He was changeable and selfish. In spite of his years he continued his bachelor life with girls. He had no home, no settled residence, no wife.

Soon the Bouviers began to separate, the members to wander far and wide. Michel Charles's vast old mansion was empty and the expense of keeping it was absurd. No one could afford to live in it. It was finally sold, and Bouviers dispersed, the family wealth scattered.

———·—●—➤—·———

Jacqueline grew up with her heart torn in three directions, her father and the Bouviers, her mother, her stepfather, kindly and stable. She was not a rebel and she accepted life as she found it, going to private schools and earning high marks, conducting herself always in the accepted ways of a young girl of social position. Vassar was her college and she continued to be a good student and to do all that was expected of her.

Outwardly conservative, almost conventionally

so, she had nevertheless a personality that compelled attention. She was a daughter of Jack Bouvier, a lover of beauty and style, with a dominance which, though quiet and controlled, somehow charmed people to devotion.

Her true life, however, was lived within herself. The confusion of her outer circumstances, the tangle of three family concerns, provided an environment, perhaps, which she could endure only by escaping into the inner world of self.

Now, when she emerges it is almost with histrionic skill. She seems not to enjoy conversation with anyone alone, but when she meets with the company of many others she makes an appearance as an actress might, an actress of taste and talent, outshining everyone present and compelling an attention she seems to enjoy.

Shyness and sensitivity are combined with ease and self-confidence in fascinating contradiction, and yet both are the inevitable results of the confusion in her life. It is perhaps the only way in which she can cope, as Rose Kennedy might put it. The truth probably is to be found in the instinctive inviolate self she feels compelled to maintain. With one person it is difficult to hide the self. In a crowd she can play a role.

In her youth there was the constant pull between her father and her mother. Jack Bouvier continued to pay her expenses and was happy when she was at college, nearer to New York than to

Washington. But she was a beautiful girl and the truth is she had very little time for either parent. When she wanted to entertain, it was easy and delightful to do so at one of her stepfather's sumptuous homes.

Then, too, he had children of her own age. As years passed, her mother had two more children. All this tended to pull her toward the Auchincloss family rather than toward her father's small apartment in New York.

His private, unacknowledged sense of failure could only be deepened as he realized that his daughter was being drawn more and more into her mother's new life. The realization embittered him to the end of his days.

There were, however, periods of affectionate closeness, notably in the year she spent in study in France, first at the University of Grenoble and then at the Sorbonne in Paris. At least she was safely away from her mother. Jacqueline seemed to enjoy the vivacious life of France and she perfected herself in the language which suited her personality.

She came home with added grace and charm and, to her father's delight, became engaged to the handsome son of a New York banker. Now she would live in New York, and they would see each other often and he could again become a part of her life. Alas, the engagement did not last and his dream ended again.

Almost before he knew it, she was talking of going back to Paris. She had won first prize in *Vogue*'s Prix de Paris contest by devising a plan for an issue of that magazine, writing four articles on high fashion and an essay on people she wished she had known. She was offered six months in the *Vogue* Paris office and six months in its New York office!

Alas, again he was disappointed and so indeed was she, for her mother and stepfather persuaded her not to accept the prize because she had been so much away from home. She, herself, was willing to forgo the prize for one reason only — she was afraid that if she went again to Paris, she would never want to leave that city of delight. Jacqueline completed her education at George Washington University.

Now her father renewed an offer he had made before, that she come and work in his office for a salary. But her stepfather came forward with a counterproposal. She had long been interested in journalism and he helped her to get a job with the *Washington Times-Herald*. She became a photographer-journalist, at first without a by-line, but attaining the distinction in a year.

In 1952, while she was at this work, she met John F. Kennedy at a dinner party. A few months later they began to see each other often. Soon there were rumors of an engagement, but she denied them because, she is said to have replied to someone's question, he was "mad enough to intend to become president."

But she became engaged to him on June 25, 1953, although, conscientious journalist that she was, she withheld the public announcement for some days until after the *Saturday Evening Post* appeared with an article entitled "Jack Kennedy: The Senate's Gay Young Bachelor."

The wedding was in September. Jack Bouvier determined to make his appearance the best of his life. Beautifully dressed, charming in manner, still handsome, he went to Newport the day before the wedding and took rooms at the best hotel. He was treated with the utmost courtesy, but the next morning as he was preparing for the wedding he was utterly unable to proceed.

Word was sent that he could not attend the wedding. It was Hugh Auchincloss who gave Jacqueline away. However deeply she may have felt her father's absence, she allowed no sign of distress to escape her. She was radiant and beautiful and the wedding was a triumph.

In the hotel Jack Bouvier packed his bags and returned to New York. His defection, at first only a rumor of illness, seeped through society gossip and he was never again the personality he had been. He withdrew from public notice and lived more and more to himself until he was alone with the two people who served him.

6

THE life of Jacqueline Bouvier after she became Jacqueline Kennedy is too well known for me to repeat it here. The Kennedy family gave her security financially and psychologically. They expected her to become a member of the family in return. Doubtless the demands that the Kennedy family made upon their son John's talented and beautiful young wife were occasionally burdensome to her, accustomed as she was to her own inner life, but in exchange she now had the security of belonging definitely with one family group.

More difficult, perhaps, was her adjustment to her husband, himself a Kennedy and therefore accustomed to the drive of a political life. The whole Kennedy family was absorbed in political affairs, international as well as national, but Jacqueline

Bouvier Kennedy was bored by politics and, she readily admitted, by politicians. Art and artists were her interest, and she may have been lonely in those years when her husband concentrated on his career as a senator and his determination to reach the presidency.

A friend of Jacqueline's confided to me that "before he married, Jack told Jackie he wanted at least five children. Every Kennedy man wants children. Jacqueline had four in seven years. He was always happiest when a baby was on the way." She had two miscarriages before Caroline was born.

I wonder, now, whether he had a presage of early death! Nature has its own communication. I remember a study made by a Brazilian scientist of note in which he wrote that where there was a presage of early death among a people the birthrate was abnormally high. He cited India as one example among others, where because of semistarvation death came early and instinct for self-preservation drove men and women to produce many children. Is it possible, therefore, that the Kennedy men, indoctrinated lifelong in ambition and consequent daring, know, although perhaps only by instinct, that they face early death?

Still another shock fell upon Jacqueline in the summer of 1957. She had seen very little of her father since her marriage, although she knew how he cherished his daughters and longed to hear from them, or, better still, see them. Unknown to her or indeed to him, he had developed cancer, and on a hot midsummer's day he died in a hospital after weeks of frightful pain.

She hastened to his side, her sister, Lee, and John Kennedy with her. But Jacqueline took charge of the funeral and insisted upon summer garden flowers, for she remembered her father as gay and lighthearted. When he was buried in East Hampton, she covered the mound with bachelor's buttons. There were few relatives at the funeral and somehow now, too late, they remembered Jack Bouvier's good qualities, how amusing he had been, how debonair, how handsome. He died without ever seeing his new grandchild, Caroline. He died before he had the joy of seeing his beloved Jacqueline become First Lady of the United States.

She took with her into the White House her inheritance from her father, her sense of style, her love of beauty, her aloofness, her dramatic ability to appear suitably her best on all public occasions. The boredom was gone. Now she really had a part to play, a part far beyond a mere senator's wife.

John Fitzgerald Kennedy had taken for his own the word *excellence,* and in her own way Jacqueline applied the word to all she did. She was essentially a homemaker. National and international affairs did not concern her, or even interest her. Wherever she was, nevertheless, she behaved with dignity and a sense of style, but she was the antithesis of Eleanor Roosevelt, who traveled far and near in her world interests. Jacqueline Kennedy, when she went abroad alone or with her husband, was always herself, beautifully dressed, composed, well-bred, but the President's wife.

She has been criticized for the cost of her wardrobe, a criticism I consider unjust and even absurd. When the demands made upon her are considered, it is evident that she was far from being extravagant. It was proper that she, a young and beautiful woman, should so represent our nation that Americans could take pride in her appearance as well as in her behavior.

Certainly it was a source of pride to me that she appeared in France simply but well dressed and that she spoke to the French people in their own tongue. And I watched her on television when she accompanied the President to South America and I shared his pride when, at his request, she stepped to the podium, dressed in a classically cut suit, wearing a pillbox hat, and spoke to the South Americans in Spanish.

I consider, moreover, that she contributed immeasurably to the dignity of our people and our capital city when she redecorated the White House, restoring so much of its original beauty at an amazingly low cost, so that now it is a work of art worthy of a great and powerful nation. In my opinion, she has indeed done more for the beauty and dignity of our country than the wife of any other president. In her own fashion she lifted our ideals. She reminded us that art is a source of spiritual power in any people. Grossness, the commonplace, even folksiness were impossible to her.

Let some call her cold, let some call her snobbish. They are wrong on both counts. She is deeply warm toward individuals she knows and trusts. She does not like crowds and crowd behavior. She maintains a suitable distance between herself and servants and employees, and in this she shows good sense. Toward their lowbred criticism and talcbearing she pays no heed.

I particularly like Robert Kennedy's appraisal of his sister-in-law whom he admired greatly: "She's poetic, whimsical, provocative, independent, and yet very feminine. Jackie has always kept her own identity and been different. That's important in a woman. What husband would want to come home at night and talk to another version of himself? Jack knows she'll never greet him with 'What's new in Laos?'"

Ethel flatly declared, "You'll have a hard time getting to the bottom of *that* barrel, which was great for Jack who was so inquisitive. The wheels go around constantly in Jackie's head. You can't pigeonhole her. Her house in Georgetown was such heaven and so supremely well organized. I always got depressed coming back to my madhouse."

And someone said, I don't know who, "She was

born first-class and never looked back to see who was traveling behind her.'' And that, too, is Jacqueline Kennedy.

Above all, she lifted the standards of American life. It was no longer a disgrace not to be "chummy" and on a first-name basis with everyone. Culture was no longer a dirty word or even dangerous. She was a skilled and charming hostess, whether to foreign royalty or to thousands of children on the White House lawn.

She made visits to various countries, she was received with curiosity, admiration, affection, always herself, never pretending to be more, or less, and carrying always the aura of a charming individual and yet inexplicable.

Nehru, the prime minister of India, received her with warmth, and for him I think she exemplified the personification of the White Goddess of Robert Graves:

"The real, perpetually obsessed Muse-poet makes a distinction between the Goddess as revealed in the supreme power, glory, wisdom and love of woman, and the individual woman in whom the Goddess may take up residence for a month, a year, seven years or even longer. The Goddess abides."

7

ALL THE world knows with what dignity and grace Jacqueline behaved in the days following the assassination, with what strength she put aside her own sorrow and thought only of being worthy of the tragic occasion, how wisely as a mother she brought her children with her all the way, yet how sensitive she was to their tender age. Who can remember without heartbreak the young widow, her children at her side, as the casket passed, and how the little three-year-old son saluted his father's passing! Who but the mother could have taught him that final gesture of love and honor?

This I shall not dwell upon, for others have done so. Let me write of what came after, the adjustment that no one could help her to make. All through the tragic days of death and funeral she had not thought of herself but only of him. Against the President's friends and associates, against the Kennedy family, she decided that as her husband had been greater than friends and family in life, so must he continue to be in death. He must be buried in the national cemetery, for he belonged to his people and his place was in the beautiful city where he had served them so well.

After the funeral was over, after the birthday party for three-year-old John was held — and what courage it took to be gay for a little boy's birthday! — after she had met alone with General de Gaulle, Eamon de Valera, and Haile Selassie, the only three with whom she chose to meet alone, she was no longer an official lady. She was a widow, she was just Mrs. John Kennedy.

It must have been a relief, a profound relief, to be no longer on stage, no longer compelled to play a part. She was alone with herself at last, that inviolate solitary company in which she had learned long ago to live. Only now she was really alone as she had never been before. She had known what love and companionship could be, the close intimate love and companionship of a dynamic man, and she had only the memory of it left, a precious memory, but that was all. What no one could supply was the physical presence, the voice, the spirit to which she had become accustomed.

Here I pause to write of what I know so well. How can one explain that adoring fans, an affectionate public, cannot assuage a widow's loneliness?

When the fan letters are answered, the concerned messages and telephone calls from loving friends are received, the day ends and the long night stretches ahead. Even the children must be in their beds and the light put out, the doors closed.

She wandered about the comfortable New York apartment she had chosen, restless and tragically alone. Her brother-in-law, Robert Kennedy, was her devoted helper with every problem, and especially with her children, but he had a wife and many children of his own. She could not depend utterly upon him.

And the public, affectionate as they were, could be and were in fact very demanding. They insisted that she be what they wanted her to be, the ideal widow of a great man, even as they had demanded that she be the ideal wife. The Image must be maintained. Even when the idea was grudgingly introduced that so young and beautiful a woman could scarcely expect never to marry again, there was almost no one they could accept — why do I say almost? *There was no one they would accept!*

In a memorial issue of LOOK magazine the widow wrote:

"It is nearly a year since he has been gone.

"On so many days — his birthday, an anniversary, watching his children running to the sea — I have thought, 'But this day last year was his last to see that.' He was so full of love and life on all

87

those days. He seems so vulnerable now, when you think that each one was a last time.

"Soon the final day will come around again — as inexorably as it did last year. But expected this time.

"It will find some of us different people than we were a year ago. Learning to accept what was unthinkable when he was alive changes you.

"I don't think there is any consolation. What was lost cannot be replaced.

"Someone who loved President Kennedy, but who had never known him, wrote to me this winter: 'The hero comes when he is needed. When our belief gets pale and weak, there comes a man out of that need who is shining — and everyone living reflects a little of that light — and stores up some against the time when he is gone.'

"Now I think that I should have known that he was magic all along. I did know it — but I should have guessed that it could not last. I should have known that it was asking too much to dream that I might have grown old with him and see our children grow up together.

"So now he is a legend when he would have preferred to be a man. I must believe that he does not share our suffering now. I think for him — at least he will never know whatever sadness might have lain ahead. He knew such a share of it in his life that it always made you so happy whenever you saw him enjoying himself. But now he will never know more — not age, nor stagnation, nor despair, nor crippling illness, nor loss of any more people he loved. His high noon kept all the freshness of the morning — and he died then, never knowing disillusionment.

> '... he has gone ...
> Among the radiant, ever venturing on,
> Somewhere, with morning, as such spirits will.'

"He is free and we must live. Those who love him must know that 'the death you have dealt is more than the death which has swallowed you.' "

"I try not to be bitter," she said then, aware that she still felt that emotion — that he who was so unvindictive toward his opponents could inspire such hatred — that she couldn't have borne more children for him . . . that the world, while remembering, tended to think of him as an "atypical" American, as if an American politician could not be civilized and literate. "I never had or wanted a life of my own," she said. "Everything centered around Jack. I can't believe that I'll never see him again. Sometimes I wake in the morning, eager to tell him something, and he's not there. . . . Nearly every religion teaches there's an afterlife, and I cling to that hope. Those three years we spent in the White House were really the happiest time for us, the closest, and now it's all gone. Now there is nothing, nothing."

When she began to go out again, only occasionally, there was the question of who could be her escort. Adlai Stevenson, her friend, a few other older men, none of them suitors, were useful to her only as friendly escorts. But there was always the return after an evening out, the return to the silent rooms, the silent servants, the sleeping children, the bedroom, so beautiful, so lonely.

Perhaps she began to ask herself, as other women have done in like circumstances, what exactly she owed the public who made such demands upon her and gave so little. For public adulation, the preservation of the Holy Image they set up and insist upon, provides no companionship. To be an Image is to be a lifeless creature. No communication is possible. The often repeated response is always the same. "Thank you so much." "I appreciate —" The Image becomes listless, the replies grow faint. The public can do nothing about the hideous empty evenings, the total solitude of the dark nights. There was no one.

And who can blame her if in desperation she joined for a brief space the jet set? The public was displeased, but, public aside, she found the "beautiful people" no more her companions than others. Wherever she was, with whatever companions, she was not able to escape the memory of the day when the man she loved was killed.

And suddenly there was another death, another tragedy. The only one who had been able to help her, her husband's younger brother, Robert Ken-

"God does not send us a cross any heavier than we can bear. How you cope is the important thing, not the events themselves."—Rose Kennedy.

Rose Kennedy and daughters at Hyannis Port in the summer of 1934. From left Eunice, Jean, Mrs. Kennedy, Patricia, Rosemary, and Kathleen.

Jacqueline Kennedy Onassis: The late Robert Kennedy described her as "poetic, whimsical, provocative, independent, and yet very feminine."

Above: Rose Kennedy with daughters Kathleen (left) and Rosemary before their presentation at the Court of St. James's in 1938.

Below: (Seated, from left) Jacqueline, John, patriarch Joseph P. Kennedy, Eunice, Jean; (standing) Edward, Ethel, Robert, Stephen Smith in 1957.

Ethel Kennedy: A mainstay and leader of the Kennedy family and influence on the lives of third-generation Kennedys.

Eunice Kennedy Shriver, her husband Sargent, and their children are typical Kennedys—teamworkers, genuinely idealistic and brilliantly intelligent.

Joan Kennedy: The beautiful blonde wife of Edward Kennedy is an able political campaigner and loyal Kennedy.

Above: French President Charles de Gaulle receiving President John F. Kennedy and Jacqueline on their triumphant 1961 Paris visit.

Below: Assassins' bullets changed the lives of Ethel and Jacqueline, but the two women will always be part of the Kennedy legend.

Rose Kennedy on the beach at Hyannis Port with her only remaining son, Edward, titular head of the Kennedy dynasty.

Above: Jean Kennedy Smith, least political of the Kennedy women, enjoys her private life and role as wife to Stephen and mother to their two children.

Below: Eunice Shriver, Ethel Kennedy, and Kennedy grandchildren swimming in Nantucket Sound, off Hyannis Port.

Jacqueline Kennedy Onassis helping John F. Kennedy, Jr., don a ski parka during family holiday at Sun Valley, Idaho.

Joan and Edward Kennedy during John F. Kennedy Regatta on Chesapeake Bay.

Kennedy widow Ethel has not allowed herself sadness nor accepted it from others.

Patricia Kennedy Lawford, only divorced Kennedy, joins sisters-in-law Joan and Ethel for family conference at 1964 Democratic convention.

Above: "This is the way we always come home from Mass," quipped Robert Kennedy on a Sunday tour of Warsaw, Poland, with Ethel in 1964.

Below: Ethel Kennedy, a symbol of motherhood, with ten of her eleven children.

Caroline Kennedy visits the Arlington grave of her father, John F. Kennedy. She has known profound tragedy and irreplaceable loss.

nedy, met the same fate. There had been a few months of revived hopefulness. She knew that, of all the men in the world whom her husband would have chosen to follow him into the presidency, his brother Robert would have been the first.

When Robert Kennedy announced his candidacy on March 16, 1968, the entire Kennedy family, including Jacqueline, took fresh courage. Now John Fitzgerald Kennedy's ideals would march on, be carried to success. Who could foretell that on June the fifth the same tragedy would repeat itself? If Ethel Kennedy was the one most bereft, Jacqueline was a close second. Rose Kennedy by now had the wisdom of her years, the stoicism of her religion. But the other two women were young, and life had not fulfilled itself.

Jacqueline, surveying her life, now so limited, only the public by day, only herself alone by night, came to the conclusion that she must marry again. Two necessities were obvious. First, she must have security for herself and then for her children. That demanded an older man, a man who had made his place in life, who could consider her tenderly first of all and take care of her, and upon whom she could lean with complete trust because he himself was secure.

Memories of her father remained. Charming

and dearly as she had loved him, he had never been
secure enough in himself to provide security for
her. And her stepfather, so trustworthy, so reliable,
had lacked perhaps the sensitivity which her artistic
nature demanded.

Second, the man she married must love children, must love her children. She was and is a good
mother. One can see that in the way her children
cling to her, depend upon her, share their play with
her. The relationship she has with Caroline is obvious. The young girl adores her mother and copies
her behavior, her actions, admires her beauty.

Jacqueline Kennedy's demands were not slight.
They were profound and searching. It would have
been hard to find the qualities she needed in any
American, and difficult even in older England. She
enjoys the French, but volatility is natural to them,
and to Italian men she appeared cool.

Greece was the country to which she had turned
more than once for pleasure and for comfort. When
her baby son, Patrick Bouvier, died in 1963 after
his short life, she had recuperated physically and
spiritually on a trip to the Aegean with her sister
Lee's friend, Aristotle Onassis. He it was, too, who
had come to her immediately after her husband's
death. Thereafter, though always quietly, he was
often her escort, and his warm Mediterranean
charm gave her comfort. Perhaps, too, it spoke to
her own Mediterranean ancestry.

They had much in common. He loved beauty, he

loved art, and he had the money to indulge her tastes. He is one of the richest men in all the world. For the rest of her life she need never again think of money nor whether she could afford something she wanted. This, too, was security. And he loves children. He has a natural ability to communicate with them. And he loves her with maturity and compassion.

"She is so like a bird," he said of her. "She wants the protection of the nest, yet she wants, as well, the freedom to fly. I offer her both." He is a wise and kind man.

When he first proposed marriage to her, she hesitated. Only when Robert Kennedy was killed did she resolve to accept Onassis. She could not live alone any longer, and now she would really be alone. There was no one in the Kennedy family who could replace in any measure the two who had been killed.

A total change of scene, a new life, was the solution, and a new life on a beautiful island in Greece. She chose, and she chose wisely, let the public think what it likes. She need never pay heed to it again.

When asked about the marriage, Rose Kennedy said, "I think she will be very happy. . . . It's been quite a lonely life for her. . . ."

Recently I sat in the living room of a lovely old house in Georgetown. The house belongs to a close friend of the Kennedy family, and it was natural that we should discuss the former First Lady, in whom we were both interested. I put the question to my friend. He was pouring a cup of tea and handed it to me. "Is Jacqueline Onassis happy, do you think?" I asked.

"Very happy," he said firmly. "I have seen them together socially and I have been with them at home. Of course they are interesting to each other. Her mind is still growing and questioning and young, and his mind much older, very wise and sophisticated.

"His sophistication fascinates her, she's much less so, you know. Her sheltered life, her natural aloofness have kept her rather young for her age. She's not really an intellectual. She's a woman of artistic tastes, decided likes and dislikes, and certainly of deep feelings — a searching sort of person.

"She's a great letter writer, by the way. Sometimes, after an evening's conversation, she'll write a letter, carrying it on for twenty pages. I had a letter from her the other day, explaining her point of view after an evening's talk.

"She thinks. And this fascinates Onassis, too. And he takes his responsibilities for Caroline and John very seriously, just as she does. He loves those two children; he helps them with their homework, and so on. She gets up and has breakfast at seven thirty every morning with the children. Of course, she may go back to bed, for all I know, but she does breakfast with them.

"It is a different sort of life for her, of course,

but satisfying. It is building new memories. She has new comforts, too, and greater luxuries than she has ever had, even in the White House. Strangely enough, she was not too comfortable there, in mere physical terms. The part of the house reserved for the family did not provide spacious living, at least for people accustomed to wealth.

"A long corridor, somewhat dark, divided the second floor where they lived. Bedrooms were on either side. An oval room, decorated in yellow, was a sort of sitting room where the family met before dinner. Another room at the opposite end was Jacqueline's own room.

"Yet the floor never seemed crowded, and the President sometimes brought his guests there. Usually the small dinner parties of six or eight guests, which, as you know, was the way she and the President liked to entertain, were served in the family dining room. The old formal dinner parties were changed to friendly informal occasions. Yet it is not easy for a president or his wife to make friends or even to know who are their friends.

" 'The presidency is not a very good place to make new friends,' John F. Kennedy once said, and Jacqueline had the frequent sadness of seeing people she had thought her friends become enemies or sycophants, so that the formal dinners grew less and less frequent, and a few old and tried friends, secure enough to need no favors, were the usual guests.''

While I ruminated, my friend went on talking.

"Caroline and John were wonderful in the White House. I remember one day that I passed them on their way somewhere, and I asked Caroline who her friend was and she replied with great dignity, 'He's not my friend. He's my brother.'"

We laughed, and I asked if the close relationship still held in the new household. He said it did, more closely, perhaps, because they are conscious of being Kennedys, although they are both fond of their stepfather.

"In fact," he said, "I feel a warmer relationship altogether in the new household, as you put it. There are not many spoken endearments between the husband and wife, but they are relaxed when they are together, and every now and again one catches an exchange of a glance between them, conveying understanding, mutual enjoyment of a joke, or a pleasure. It's rather nice."

This, too, set my wondering alive again. Perhaps the wife needed a husband who was old enough to treasure her, to understand her, to be tender with her, to want her to be herself. Young husbands think of themselves first, and wives are helpers and adjuncts and followers. They must think first of their husbands.

But the young wife of a much older husband is his joy and his darling, a combination of daughter, mistress, and wife. His desire is to see her happy and indulged and, therefore, pleased with him. Yes,

Jacqueline Onassis has chosen well for herself. She is secure, and security in this age and in this world is enough — or almost enough — is it not? At least, it is very rare.

Recently, in an obscure small newspaper in my small Vermont town, a rag of a newspaper but one which people devour, I read an article reporting, or purporting to report, the influence that Jacqueline Onassis is having upon her husband, Aristotle Onassis. According to the article, she is changing this man from a shrewd accumulator of vast wealth to a philanthropist. Until now, so the report runs, Onassis had not believed in charity. He had maintained that people should be able to take care of themselves. Now, under the influence of this strong, beautiful woman, he is changing the image he has built for himself through the years. He is giving large sums of money to help unfortunate persons, especially children. An institution he financed in Greece has been named Onassion in his honor. Moreover, he has yielded to his wife's desire to rear her two Kennedy children in their own country. He lives in New York, as she wishes, only visiting his beloved island home in Greece, and he has given up entirely his lavish apartment in Paris.

His wife has actually brought this self-centered aging man into the aura of the Kennedy legend, a legend in which she herself was not reared, but which she must have absorbed from her Kennedy husband. The legend has become a part of her now.

She has not allowed herself to change, and is maintaining the legend and extending its influence to include one of the richest men in the world. She seemed to have lost this position of influence when she married Onassis. People then were outspoken in their disappointment. They felt she had violated the legend, had indeed almost betrayed it. But now, the exhibition of such strength, such maintenance of her own independent faithfulness to the legend, is fast restoring to her the position she once held.

———•◆•◆•———

Among the Kennedy women, Caroline Kennedy is old enough to be included. She is too young, of course, for us to know how the tragic and extraordinary events of her life have affected or will yet affect her. Her earliest memories are of the White House, and her life there was at once privileged and, in some ways, disadvantaged by privilege. She was then a lovely, spontaneous little girl. Her father's death gave her an early acquaintance with the tragedy that seems endemic in the Kennedy family. Today she is almost a teen-ager, extraordinarily beautiful and instinctively elegant. She has had the example of her mother, of course. I see how precisely Caroline places her feet together, how she holds herself and with what cool dignity presents herself to the public, in unconscious — or perhaps conscious — imitation of the mother she adores.

Now, as Aristotle Onassis's stepdaughter, it is inevitable that Caroline, reared in regal surroundings, will have her own contribution to make to the future. She has every so-called advantage. But she has something of her own that money cannot buy nor inheritance bestow. She has had experience, cruelly young, of profound tragedy and irreplaceable loss. She has already learned that life does not spare the beautiful and the privileged.

Whatever the future holds for Caroline Kennedy, it cannot fail to present its own extremes of joy and sorrow. Her destiny will carry her high and may bring her low. The sensitivity inherent in her nature will give her joy yet make her suffer to a degree far beyond the ordinary measure. But she is no common child. She is a Kennedy and she inherits, too, the Kennedy courage.

8

THE ELDEST living Kennedy daughter, after Rosemary, is Eunice, whom I know through our mutual interest in mental retardation. When I visited her home in Washington, D.C., her husband, Sargent Shriver, was then head of the newly founded Peace Corps.

I remember, when I entered the house the first time, that the atmosphere seemed one of activity, of engagement, of concern. I sat alone in the pleasant living room, waiting for my hostess. Wide glass doors opened to a terrace and beyond was a spacious green lawn encircled by trees. I had the feeling that somehow a good deal had been going on that day, an atmosphere characteristic of the Kennedys, and when my hostess came in, a little late and somewhat hurried, she explained that a crowd of retarded children had been there to play on the lawn and enjoy the grounds. As I remember, it was a special summer school for such children, and I thought how wonderfully kind it was of a busy woman to entertain these children in so generous a manner.

She was very typical of the Kennedy family, I thought, as I listened to her account of the day's activities, a day crowded with events for her husband's work as well as her own. Each member of the Kennedy family has, it seems, a special sphere of family responsibility. For Eunice Shriver, it is the area of mental retardation and she has represented the family ably.

She is a striking-looking woman, forthright, vigorous, honest, and highly intelligent without being an intellectual in the theoretical sense. She has the Kennedy directness, the Kennedy energy, the Kennedy accent.

She is the most typical of the Kennedy women and one who, had she been born a generation or two later, would certainly have found politics her field. At the time of this writing, it has been mentioned in the news that Sargent Shriver will actively enter politics. If he does, his wife will be his greatest political asset. Brilliant, fearless, imaginative in her ideas and purposes, she will be a strength in herself.

I remember the first time she spoke to me. It was by telephone. The instant I heard her voice, I recognized it. That is a Kennedy, I told myself.

"Pearl Buck? This is Eunice Shriver. I want —"

I enjoyed the air of involvement, excitement, accomplishment, that was everywhere in Eunice's home. Sargent Shriver came in on time for dinner, a pleasant, intelligent man, relaxed in manner, a foil for his high-strung wife.

The Kennedy women who have married have not made easy wives. Their husbands have had to remain strong men. Sargent Shriver, seemingly so easygoing, seemingly so casual that he recently forgot or apparently forgot an important ambassadorial reception in our own embassy in Paris, is only apparently easygoing and casual. He wins his battles by his own methods. To see him with Eunice, his wife, is to learn how he does it. Obviously he loves her, obviously he understands her, he is always courteous, a gentleman born, always fair, always ready to hear her arguments, and yet one knows that his decisions are his own. He is pleasantly invincible.

There is an air of perfect understanding between the Shrivers, each allowing the other to speak without interruptions — no slight accomplishment for American men and their wives, as I have observed, one or the other is usually a born interrupter. Between Eunice and her husband, however, there is mutual consideration and respect.

Once I had occasion to visit Sargent Shriver in his office on business and, again, I was impressed by his patience in hearing me out, his quick understanding of the situation I was there to explain, his readiness to advise and to help. I felt a Kennedy influence there, although I am sure his own nature is sympathetic.

The instinct of all the Kennedys and their mates is to help where help is needed. Even Joseph Kennedy, Sr., that doughty fighter for his own rights, had many secret charities. Rueful experience taught him not to expect gratitude, of course, and he learned that hard lesson so well, in fact, that he made a wry quip about it.

"Every good deed brings its own punishment," he said. He established another Kennedy habit, too. He made his charities secret. People lived half a lifetime without knowing that he was paying their salaries or contributing to their work. He did not want such persons to know of his charity lest they be robbed of self-respect. There were those who thought of him as a hard, bargain-driving man, and there was that man in him as there is something of those qualities in every Kennedy, but they are balanced by great generosity in giving as well as in understanding.

———

Eunice, I know, gave much love and companionship and joy to her older sister, Rosemary. Joe was four years old and Jack only three when Rosemary was born. Eunice had not yet arrived. Rose was twenty-eight and blooming with good health. There was no problem in the baby's delivery.

Rosemary was beautiful, like her mother. She proved to be slow at accomplishing the normal little achievements children do in early development. But her brothers were considered so "advanced" that little attention was paid to her backwardness. Doctors said she would suddenly start performing normally. But she didn't. It was finally faced. Rosemary was mentally retarded.

As I have said, Rose and Joseph Patrick refused to put her into an institution. The father insisted that anything that could be done for her in an institution could be done as well at home.

As young Joe and Jack grew and other babies came, Rosemary also grew. She was strong and lovely physically, but she remained a child mentally.

The family indeed did everything a loving family could do to make life happy and full for the girl. She did everything she was told to do. Perhaps this was her way of returning their love.

As she grew, her life presented more serious problems. She could not keep up with teen-agers of her generation. Her brothers would dance with her at parties, and they had taught her to dance well. But other boys did not cut in, or ask her to dance, and her eyes asked, "Why?" How could she be answered?

She enjoyed pretty dresses and having her hair done, and she enjoyed being with people. But, alas, people, other than her family, avoided her.

Ambassador Joseph P. Kennedy and his wife

took Rosemary with them to London and they were all presented, along with Kathleen, to the King and Queen!

But in 1941, back home, it became quite apparent that Rosemary was retrogressing rather than improving. She was becoming quarrelsome and very difficult to manage. She became sullen and withdrew and her attention span diminished.

Rose had doctor after doctor examine her. Each said the same thing: She would be better off in a home where competition would be less and she would live with others of her own capacity.

A Roman Catholic institution was suggested and agreed upon, and there Rosemary Kennedy has found peace.

One summer day when I was in my Vermont house, where I am at this instant of writing, the desk telephone rang. I lifted the receiver and again recognized the unmistakable Kennedy voice and accent. It was indeed Eunice Shriver.

This time there was something she wanted me to do for her. It was to write an introduction for a book which was in fact a report on abortions when it is fairly certain that if a child is allowed to be born, it will be retarded. I had firm views on the subject and I was pleased that she did not ask me what those views were. I assumed that as a Roman Catholic she would probably not approve of abortions, but I, too, did not inquire. I was happy to do what she asked me to do. As it happened, we were in agreement, although I felt she would have accepted disagreement, honest soul that she is.

Eunice Kennedy was, of course, very useful in political campaigns for her brothers because of her organizational skills. With her sisters, Patricia and Jean, she helped make a success of the enjoyable 1952 tea parties. She toured during Jack's other campaigns and was a forceful, effective speaker in her husband's home state, Illinois.

There is a strong family likeness in all the members of the Kennedy family, a similarity. Every Kennedy has style, force, personality; whatever it may be called, it is a characteristic common to them all.

When one of them enters a room, it is with a presence, inexplicable except that it is visible and undeniable, an emanation of a family personality, a combination of determination, ambition, idealism, and a general joyousness which is singularly attractive. These traits are balanced to a degree by impatience, intolerance, and a sense of self-importance.

The Kennedy women are all feminine, but it is obvious that they are feminine in the modern, horseback-riding, tennis-playing fashion. None of them is a humble housewife. They are independent but considerate, efficient as a matter of course but careless of praise, ambitious but not personally so. They are team workers, and the entire family, in which they include their successful husbands, is the team. They are more concerned about family approval than with public acceptance.

None of the Kennedy women fulfill this role better than Eunice Shriver. Hardworking, brilliantly intelligent, genuinely idealistic, she is at the same time feminine. Her slender frame is taut as a coiled spring, time is always too short for her many activities, her life is planned and has to be. She carries on a complex life and has done so for years. She is an affectionate but an efficient mother, a devoted wife but one with her own work for which she is responsible. She is more than competent in her many roles.

In Sargent Shriver she chose a man eminently suited to join the family team. Energetic and idealistic, he built in the Peace Corps an organization that expressed well the spirit of President Kennedy's term of service. It will undoubtedly receive less attention and publicity during the Nixon administration, but its formation was part of the Kennedy administration's "caring for people." And the accomplishments of the Peace Corps are inestimable.

The Shriver children are independent, for they carry the Kennedy genes. They are amazingly modest, they take for granted their distinguished family background, and they will make their own place in the world without needing to boast of who they are. As part of the Kennedy family, they accepted without astonishment the fact that one of their number was president of the United States. They paid him proper respect but he was still their uncle. When he was assassinated, they took it for granted that another Kennedy would take his place. That brother, of course, was Uncle Bob — Robert Francis Kennedy.

9

ROBERT Kennedy was a fascinating complexity. I knew that the first time I met him. We met by appointment in his offices in the Old Senate Office Building in Washington, D.C. It was strictly a business meeting. I had gone there to ask a favor of him. It was to request him to join the board of governors of the organization I was setting up on behalf of the Amerasians — that is, the children of American servicemen in Asia and Asian women.

His offices were totally different from a visit, two years later, to his younger brother's offices. Robert Kennedy's offices were quiet and orderly, almost empty. Without delay I was ushered into the room where, solitary, he sat behind his desk. It was a huge room, sparsely but tastefully furnished, and the desk was proportionately even more huge, so huge that it dwarfed the figure seated behind it.

I saw a rather small man, or he appeared small, a young man whose face was somber but whose eyes were a burning blue. Were they really blue? Or were they so intense that now I think of them as blue? At any rate, they were unsmiling and he did not smile.

I spoke my piece, I made my request. He listened carefully, his expression unchanging. I waited for his reply. It was a flat no. He was busy. He did not like to lend the use of his name. It sounded like a good cause, but there were many good causes. His family had undertaken the cause of retarded children. He half rose from his chair, signifying that there was no more to be said. He was abrupt and made no ado as to courtesy. I, however, had come with a purpose, and I, too, can be persistent.

"Mr. Kennedy," I said, "I need your name because people in Asia trust you. If they see that you are interested in these new people, the Amerasians, they will take thought, and perhaps realize that consideration should be given to the situation and therefore do their share in solving a real problem.

"The Amerasians are stateless, Mr. Kennedy. We Americans consider them Asians, but in Asia the child belongs to the father and so in Asia they are considered Americans. The consequence is that they are stateless. They have no country, no government. They are alien in the lands where they are born."

He was too courteous to leave the room, and I

held him there, refusing to go until I had made my case. He sat down again. He listened. I watched those burning eyes fixed on my face. He did not interrupt me. When I had finished, he said abruptly:

"I will think it over and write you."

"Thank you," I said and left.

I suppose he wanted to consult with his family, for of course the Kennedy name did not belong to him alone. In a few days his letter reached me. It brought his consent. His name on our letterhead still gives me strength, although he is dead.

Robert Kennedy was the third among four sons. Physically he was the smallest in stature and yet, to me, he was the most dramatic in appearance. I suppose in strict assessment he was the least handsome, and yet he was the most dynamic. When he came into the room one felt a personality, changeable, moody, humorous in a wry fashion, able to laugh at himself, but I am not sure how easily he accepted the laughter of others.

Since he was the smallest of the Kennedy sons, he learned to "fight tough," to be belligerent, to be relentless with himself and fearless everywhere. He was not suave in manner. He said what he thought and bluntly. Conciliation was not his technique. Yet he could be kind almost to sentimentality when he was moved.

He was a complex man, or, as has been said, a compound of several simple men. Whatever he was at the moment, he was altogether that man. With children he was wholeheartedly at play, and yet in an instant he could become the stern father. His temper could flash, and yet he could receive criticism with cold, unchanging endurance.

Morally he was almost puritanical, the moral imperative his habit of mind. Because of a certain rigidity in his nature, he invited attack. And yet in his beliefs he was left of the center, never accepting conservatism for the sake of being conservative. Principle was his guiding star, but principle changed with enlightenment. He was not a black-and-white man. And he had in him depths of compassion for the young, the honest, the searching, for these were his own qualities.

Above all, he had spirit; dashing, exciting. He was a born leader, sure of himself, arbitrary yet capable of reason. People loved him or hated him. He cared for neither love nor hate when he was pursuing in his relentless way a principle, a task, to which he was devoted. And yet I discerned a pervading sensitivity in this man, thin-skinned perceptivity which he endeavored to hide, a secret pain which he was resolved never to acknowledge or even to recognize.

He was not soft with himself. There was no softness in him anywhere. It was pleasant, on the other hand, to see this impetuous, energetic, occasionally ruthless man change into a playful young father with his children.

His house teemed with children, ten, with an eleventh on the way when he died. To his own, he

added the two his president brother had left behind.
He had an affinity with the young. They adored him
and followed him. He played with them but he
played hard.

Whether people loved or detested Robert Kennedy, he had the Kennedy magic. People thronged
about him, they wanted to touch him, a virtue, in the
old biblical sense, flowed from him, and this though
he made no effort in their direction. He was careless
of their opinion, he had no small talk, in conversation the other person had to do the talking, he might
reply and he might not. And yet, a deep understanding of a child, or an old person, or someone dying in
extremity, welled from him upon occasion.

One aspect of Robert Kennedy's performance
which was difficult to understand was his connection
with Joseph McCarthy. Perhaps it was inexperience
and immaturity that prevented Bobby from grasp-
ing the implications of Senator McCarthy's ill-in-
formed attacks, and the endless damage they did to
many a good and loyal American. His brother John
Kennedy, always impatient with Senator McCarthy's antics, was not only older but had been matured
by illness and heroic encounter with life and death.

Robert Kennedy was at once simple and sophisticated. He did not have the intellectual and literary
background his brother, the president, had. He
tended to command rather than to persuade. He did
not hide his will to win. In some ways, he was more
like his father than the others were. Yet he was not

self-important. His interest was not in drawing attention to himself but in getting the work done. He despised laziness and dilatoriness and lack of organization. Yet he was sophisticated enough to realize his own position. He accepted deference as a matter of course. When he boarded the family plane, he expected it to take off as soon as he was on.

A complex of contradictions, it is difficult to imagine what he might have become had he lived. Certainly he had not reached the height of his capacity. It seems true that the more capacity a human being has for growth, the more slowly he — or she — matures. The shallower the mind, the more mediocre the intelligence, the earlier it reaches its capacity.

Robert Kennedy was still in the instinctive stage. He was only beginning to be interested in the intellectual, the philosophic aspects of thought. He was still far from the level of John Fitzgerald Kennedy. Perhaps the elder brother had not only had more time but more leisure in which to read, to live the life of the mind, because he was ill so often.

Robert Kennedy lived a vigorous physical life and in that life the mind slumbers and thought is stilled. It was characteristic of this younger brother that when he felt frustration, impatience, competitive determination to win, he expressed himself in violent physical exertion.

After his brother's assassination, he forced himself to climb a dangerous mountain in order to prove his own courage, express his own need to win. It was the old family spirit, an exhibition of self-discipline and power to win over self. For if he drove his staff, he drove himself most of all. Perhaps this is why they served him so loyally, in spite of his demands.

———•—•—•———

What sort of woman did this man marry? Ethel Skakel Kennedy lives at Hickory Hill in McLean, Virginia, not far from Washington, in a big comfortable family home with a bright red, welcoming front door. It is the home she shared with her husband.

I know that Robert Kennedy loved his wife deeply and completely. He loved her for to him she was wholly lovable. And she is woman enough to have put him first, above all, above house and friends and even above children. She understood him. She knew that he needed stability, he needed to know where she was, and so she stayed at home where he wanted her to be.

She once said, "I don't think a politician's wife should get involved in politics. I think she should work at making her home a nice place for her husband to come home to, a place for him to forget politics."

Bobby could be an ideal father, playing and romping with his children, advising and talking with them, but there were also times when he had to forget them, and he could forget them, knowing that she was there.

She believes children should be given as happy a childhood as parents can possibly give them. "When they grow up," she says, "life is difficult enough. Our children, thank God, had so many extra advantages. We tried to instill in them the realization that when they grow up, they will have to contribute to society. They learn how to do it by looking out for each other, by helping each other."

She is not a subtle woman; she is unaffected, outgoing, friendly, cheerful. Even when she is ill, she does not complain, and did not even to her husband. If she is angry, which is seldom, she speaks her mind and then forgets it. She is a wholesome woman and not manipulative. I cannot imagine her using sex as a weapon or a reward, as so many women do. She is as wholesome about motherhood as she is about everything else, especially, perhaps, as she was as a wife.

She knew that her husband had many interests, although his political life and ambitions were foremost. She did not resent his love of sports and shared it when she could. She accepted the fact that men needed the company of other men and she was not jealous of his men friends or of other women. She knew she was essential to him and that sufficed her. She never played the martyr. When he came home, it was not to be met by her with a list of her troubles and complaints. She solved her own problems and shared with him only those she could not solve alone. She had no need for the love and approval of others; she wanted only his.

When he was abroad, he sent her a love message every day in the language of each country in which he visited. She treasured, as any woman would, such spontaneous evidences of his devotion, but if he had not sent them she would not have been troubled. They were a truly married man and woman, and they enjoyed having children, many children. She liked being pregnant by him. She welcomed having a child by him. She was proud of it.

Of course she knew the danger in which he lived. She knew that if he went on to the presidency he would probably be killed. She lived in terror, but she would not let him see it. She would not let any of us see it. She had already learned to cope with tragedy: Both parents and her favorite brother, George, Jr., had been killed in freak plane accidents, and eight months later, his wife, Joan Patricia, choked to death at dinner. Ethel, indeed, knew tragedy.

She went about her own busy life in the big houseful of children, happy, occupied, cheerful, always approving of him, always encouraging him to do what he wished, as he wished to do it.

But secretly she prepared herself for whatever might happen. She knew, and she planned how she would take it and what she would do. She would continue their family life exactly as it was at Hickory Hill, only he, of course, would not be there. The children must not forget him. His pictures, his things, must not be put away. They must be left as they were, as though he were still there.

Meanwhile, she enjoyed every moment of her life with him. She traveled with him as often as she could, between pregnancies. In 1961 the President sent her with her husband to the celebration of the Ivory Coast's first year of independence, and she spoke French as she remembered it from her school days and laughed with the people when they laughed at her. They liked her self-forgetful, friendly ways.

The next year the President sent them on a worldwide goodwill tour. The Soviet Union invited them to visit Russia, but this was declined. Elsewhere the visits were highly successful and Ethel enjoyed herself.

In Italy she was given a motor scooter by American correspondents, with which she had a slight mishap with a Fiat. In Thailand she annoyed the man the State Department had sent with them by not having her bags packed on time, and gave him a peace offering. She was happy, for she was with her husband.

Home again the usual joyous life went on. The household had frequent guests, all entertained with the same informal ease. She was dubbed by her friends ''Homemaker of the Year,'' although she cannot cook. But she did not need to cook, there was always someone to do it for her. She employed eleven servants. She made everyone comfortable. She kept them amused and at ease.

Once when the Duchess of Devonshire was at Hickory Hill for luncheon, Ethel said grace and added, "And please, dear God, make Bobby buy me a bigger dining room table."

And all the time, of course, she knew. She had begun to think of it in the days after the President had been killed. She saw her husband's spirit weaken. He seemed physically to droop and fade. He grew thin, his clothes hung on him. He went for long lonely walks, accompanied only by his big dog, Brumus.

He never really talked much, but now he was exceptionally silent. He devoted himself almost fanatically to Jack's widow and children. He displayed an open prejudice against his brother's successor, Lyndon Johnson. But she understood and loved him more than ever, if that was possible, because she knew. When he decided to run for the presidency, she was certain.

". . . Your Eminences, Your Excellencies, Mr. President. In behalf of Mrs. Kennedy, her children, the parents and sisters of Robert Kennedy, I want to express what we feel to those who mourn with us today in this cathedral and around the world . . ."

The date was June 8, 1968. The place was New York's St. Patrick's Cathedral. The voice was the voice of Edward Moore Kennedy. Ethel Kennedy, dressed in mourning, a black veil over her face, listened, her children with her. She had thought herself prepared. She had known death before, sudden death. But nothing had really prepared her — nothing.

———•—•—•———

Now that he is gone, she carries on for him in her own way. She speaks out more frankly than ever for the things her husband fought for. Though she is only forty-one years old, she is still married to Robert Kennedy. She is a loyal Kennedy. But she is resolutely herself, too. Her life is planned. She is not introspective, she will not allow herself sadness, nor accept it from others. Her occupation is her children.

She is accustomed to a large family, for she was next to the youngest in a family of seven. Her Dutch father was a self-made man who began as a railway clerk and never forgot the fact. Her mother was a busy, cheerful Irishwoman. Perhaps it was from these sources that Ethel Kennedy inherited and learned her firm, practical, friendly ways.

In spite of the big house, in spite of the acres of landscape surrounding it, in spite of her many children, her life is relatively simple. She breakfasts early, at seven, with her children. She drives some of them to school, she bathes and feeds the baby, Rory. She lunches with some of her children, she reads to them.

She has many friends. Hordes of celebrities used to come to Hickory Hill when Bobby lived. Some still do. Ethel calls these show business stars "sparklies." She now makes it an unbreakable rule not to visit the Kennedy graves with any celebrity. She visits her dead only privately.

She is deeply religious, as Rose Kennedy is, and she reads the Bible to her children. In fact, there are similarities between the two women, a quality which expresses itself in fortitude. Its source, I think, is religion. "I don't know about religion as a national or political issue," Rose Kennedy once said, "but I think religion is wonderful for children. Most children seek this stability and purpose."

Again it may be that both women by nature have these qualities of stability and purpose, and simply express them through the religious atmosphere in which they have been reared. Whatever the source, the fact remains that both women profess the Roman Catholic faith, both practice it earnestly in their daily lives, both teach it to their children. And their faith gives them courage to accept life as it comes to them without despair.

10

*P*ATRICIA and Jean Kennedy were the last two of five daughters and after them there was only one more child in Joseph Patrick Kennedy's family, a son, Edward. The two younger daughters were smoothly welded into the family, parts of the whole, and as they grew they too did their share in supporting their brothers in political campaigns.

Patricia married the handsome English actor, Peter Lawford, and Jean married Stephen Smith, a capable businessman who now looks after the family interests.

Patricia's marriage, after eleven years and four children, three sons and one daughter, has ended in divorce.

As much as Peter respected Pat's family, he never became a part of it. And, as he could not enter her world, she could never leave it.

The Chinese, centuries ago, decided that the wife does not and must not continue as a member of her father's family — does not, because her heart should follow her husband and his responsibilities and obligations become hers, and must not, because a man should be able to control his wife, and if she can, at any time she is crossed, "go home to mother," then her mother is really in control. Moreover, there is no room in any family for two mothers-in-law, therefore the only mother-in-law admissible, to the Chinese way of thinking, is the husband's mother, whom, since he must obey her in proper respect, his wife must also obey.

Some years ago, in fact before Communists took control in China, I amused myself and American audiences by making a comparison of Chinese and American humor. This I did by listing comparable jokes, and discovering thereby what our two peoples laughed at.

I found that we made fun of the same sorts of persons, absentminded scholars, pretentious artists, doctors so unskilled that they kill more than they cure, and so on. There was only one type of person at whom Americans laugh who was totally lacking in the encyclopedia of Chinese humor. It was the man's mother-in-law, his wife's mother, and she was not there because she did not exist. Long ago she had been eliminated as a burden no man ought to bear. Therefore a Chinese wife is not permitted to leave her home — that is, her husband's home — whenever she likes. There are, or rather were, stated periods, once a year or so, when she might return to her father's home for a short visit. But no Chinese woman would think of being so presumptuous, so ill-mannered, as to visit her daughter's husband's house. As a consequence, no jokes about her are necessary. The husband has no relationship to his wife's mother-in-law, subject to her will and whim.

Patricia and Jean Kennedy are American, however, and it is not likely that they would even know the traditional Chinese philosophy, much less follow it. I merely put it here to suggest that perhaps the Chinese, wise in the ways of human nature, have hit upon a natural fact, that if a marriage is to last, there can be only one family to be considered, and that is the husband's family.

There was parental opposition from both sides to Patricia's and Peter's engagement. English-born Peter Sydney Ernest Lawford is the son of the late Lieutenant General Sir Sydney Lawford and Lady Lawford.

Patricia is the second youngest of the Kennedy daughters, the most attractive, the least dominating, the most yielding and gentle. Yet Lady Lawford implied that she would rather have her son marry an English girl, a girl with a title, perhaps, almost any girl, in fact, but a Kennedy girl.

Patricia's father was equally unenthusiastic about the union. He did not approve of actors for sons-in-law. He most emphatically did not approve of English actors.

Regardless, Patricia and Peter were wed in

Manhattan at the little Church of St. Thomas More, at Park Avenue and Eighty-ninth Street, on April 25, 1954. They were divorced eleven years later in Gooding, Idaho. It was the first divorce in the Roman Catholic Kennedy family.

Pat and Peter seemed for years to have a quietly happy marriage. Not even a newspaper reporter appears to know why it ended.

Peter Lawford first met Jack Kennedy at the late Gary Cooper's home in 1946, long before he met Patricia, and from the first was impressed by Jack's magnetism and drive. In 1949 he met Patricia, who was then in Hollywood, working for NBC and Kate Smith.

"Frankly, I had never known a family like the Kennedys," he admits. He was an only child, somewhat introverted, tutor taught, with all the traditional British reserve. Home to him was wherever the billets of his father took him and his mother.

"The rough-and-tumble of a large gregarious family was thus completely foreign to me, and I became — by marriage — an outsider in an almost overwhelming situation."

The Kennedys were wise in handling the situation. They were devoted to Pat and knew that Peter adored her, so they left each door ajar and waited for Peter to walk through it. They never forced their political and religious concepts on him. He wasn't even pushed into their touch football games.

"Actually it took two years of exposure to the

Kennedy family *esprit* before I began to get the message that the secret was participation. After Pat's father finally 'accepted' me, it was he who clued me in.

"He was an old movie hand himself; back in 1927, he was a motion picture executive, and show business wasn't way out to him. Since he had always been the center of family activities, encouraging his children to join in the fun and competition, he did his best to ease me in." But, apparently, Peter did not ease in too well.

When Pat married Peter, an engaging man with an actor's charm and temperament, she must have known that an artist has his own world in which he lives and he never leaves this world wholly to enter another.

Even a Kennedy cannot change an artist. Of all unreachable, unchangeable persons, the artist is the first, for he can escape any situation, any person, simply by withdrawing into his own world. His is a world entirely different from the Kennedy world in which both men and women are doers rather than creators, and they lead by positive action.

The artist is a creator, he does not seek to lead. He only offers that which he has created, to be accepted or rejected, and, whether accepted or rejected, he moves on to fresh creation, but always within his own realm.

Peter Lawford could not become part of "the Clan." He said, "Being related to the President of the United States is a very great honor. But it is not and never will be a career. When the Kennedys take you to heart, you become one of them all the way. My four children will never be loners. They are full-fledged members of the Tribe.''

———••••———

In Jean Kennedy Smith's case, however, it is different. Stephen Smith has a quiet strength of his own. His family ''had money'' long before the Kennedys knew the advantages of wealth. Without losing his own personality, he has used his talents and experience to serve the Kennedy family and its discuss.

He is dedicated to the Kennedy family although he is neither an idealist nor a crusader. He is the nonpolitical member of a political family. In an odd fashion, he is like Joseph Patrick Kennedy in that he made it possible for the Kennedy men to be political powers.

He was a young business executive, already successful, when he married Jean Kennedy in 1956. Jean Smith, blue-eyed and dark-haired, is the least political of the Kennedy women, and enjoys her home and its privacy. She is a good mother to her children and a good wife to her handsome, extremely intelligent young husband — so shrewd a business brain, by the way, that a year after his marriage his father-in-law invited him to manage and expand the

Kennedy oil interests. Now he manages the Kennedy portfolio of investments of more than three hundred million dollars, which he charmingly refuses to discuss.

He fits well into the Kennedy family, for he is also an excellent athlete, admitted even by the family to be the best all-around sportsman of them all, in golf, tennis, skiing, and even touch football!

He has, of course, been superbly successful in managing Kennedy campaigns. So far he has not shown inclinations to enter politics, although there are those among his friends who say that, whatever the topic of conversation, he always brings it around to politics. I have heard it reported, at least, that Smith himself says, "There's no fuller use of your faculties than politics." His wife is a true Kennedy woman and believes that if he did go into politics, he could of course succeed. One's own feeling is that, after the tragedies which have befallen the family, Stephen Smith will continue to be what he is: the extremely successful, dedicated manager of the family fortune, hopefully providing power for the members of the next generation of Kennedys again to make their mark as leaders in our national life.

11

OF THIS generation of Joseph and Rose Kennedy's children, there remains of their four sons only Edward. The assassination of two of his brothers has brought him into unenviably early prominence. He has gallantly stepped forward as the head of the family.

When Ethel Kennedy's eleventh child was born, he was the man at hand. Three generations of the Kennedy family now look to him as their leader.

The Kennedy children are still too young to assume responsibility. Who will teach them the strong Kennedy doctrine of family unity and the will to win? Is Edward Kennedy strong enough, mature enough, or, for that matter, is any young man able to head a family of three generations?

It is a formidable task. Given time, a man grows into the task as son, husband, father, and grandfather. But Edward Kennedy has had in a few years to assume the total burden, and to maintain it now. He has also to be the business head of family financial concerns, while he carves out his own political career — all at the same time. Under favorable circumstances and in a friendly public environment, these responsibilities might be assumed successfully, but the circumstances are not favorable and the public environment is hostile.

When individuals appear in public life with attributes and material possessions far beyond our own, it is difficult for the average man to judge them objectively or even to be just to them. The tendency in our society to be less than just to the specially gifted is a dangerous one and we lose thereby. But more of this later. I mention this characteristic here because it is pertinent to the Kennedy family at the moment, and the results fall most heavily on Edward Kennedy. With his older brothers gone, an accumulation of criticism rests upon him.

His first handicap is a personal one for which he is certainly not to blame. To be the youngest child in a family is always a handicap and certainly this is true if the family is a large one. The youngest is specially favored and unconsciously babied, and this develops in him a tendency to count upon favoritism instead of personal achievement.

At the same time he develops a doubt of his own ability in competition with his older brothers and sisters. Between being the favorite and wanting so to be, and yet wanting to prove himself worthy in his own right, we have the foundation for an insecure, wavering personality.

In Edward Kennedy's case the dichotomy is plain. He is emotionally moved by the high ideals his father and mother set for their children. But other, contradictory forces stemming from his position in the family group have made it difficult for him to develop the self-discipline necessary for the required achievement.

Self-discipline is the hardest of all disciplines. It is tested in moments of crisis when, faced by a desperate dilemma, one becomes heroic — or one becomes a coward. There was nothing of the coward in the three older brothers. Whether this is true also of Edward Kennedy cannot be known. I am sure that he himself does not know.

For it is not a simple question. He has duties and responsibilities whatever the answer. The threat of almost certain assassination if he continues his political career toward the presidency might, if he gives up this career, brand him a coward.

On the other hand, his responsibilities as the sole remaining son of the family, who must be its head and assume the position of father to sixteen children, give him not only excuse but real obligation to continue in life. The decision must be his alone and will be. The discipline and idealism of this family are such that not one member, I feel sure, will attempt to influence him, even his wife.

It has been a long time since I have thought of the Kung family in Peking. I have said that we Americans are unjust to our gifted men and women, to our outstanding families. That is true also in China.

I remember a week-long visit that I once made to the Kung family's country estate. It was summer, a beautiful day, the air so clear that the distant mountains seemed near. Madame Kung decided upon a walk and, accompanied by a suitable number of daughters-in-law and bondmaids, we sauntered outside the great vermilion gate. After half an hour or so we passed a deep ditch by the side of the road. Madame Kung pointed to it with her bamboo cane.

"That ditch," she said, "is where my parents and I hid when our peasants rebelled against us. They wanted to own our land. But the imperial armies saved us."

She appeared lost in memory for a moment and I did not disturb her. Then she sighed.

"Doubtless I and my family will hide there again one of these days. The poor always hate the rich."

Her prophecy came true. Years later when the Communists took power they vented their peasant anger against the rich, the successful, the powerful, and the Kung family was at their mercy. Alas, there were no imperial armies to save them, for the day of empire was ended and the peasants, ignorant and angry, were in power.

The Kennedy Women

Madame Kung and her husband were hanged from the painted beams of their vast ancestral hall, and their sons and sons' wives were shot. The grandchildren were taken away and put into Communist orphanages. The peasants looted the ancient house of its treasures and the land was given to a commune.

Thus ended a great family of Peking. They were too rich, too powerful, too successful, the men too handsome, their wives too beautiful, and so by the hatred of peasants and common folk they were destroyed.

Will the Kennedy "dynasty" in the United States be destroyed? The answer waits upon Edward Kennedy's decision. Has he the power to lead the young Kennedy males to greatness? I have used the word *great* so frequently in this Kennedy appraisal. But quite realistically we no longer have any truly great men in the world. Where are they? Where are the towering men in government, in science, in literature and the arts, even in the military? Where are the leaders in thought and action?

Tragically, we have suffered two world wars. The most serious loss in war is not in money, but in the death of the brave, the brilliant, the necessary men. I use the word *necessary* advisedly, for human progress depends upon extraordinary men. There are not many of them born. They are dangerously few in proportion to the total population. But they are the leaders in war as well as in peace, they are the brave, the courageous, the resourceful, the dar-

137

ing, and since they lead to battle, they take the brunt of danger, and die first.

For two generations the world has been at war in one way or another, in one place or another, and every nation so involved is feeling the result of the loss of leadership — feeling it politically but also in every aspect of national life.

We have competent, useful men who do their best to deal with events, but no men big enough to shape them. Nor can we expect much improvement in the future, for the potential leaders who died too young on battlefields everywhere in the world would have been the fathers of sons like themselves. Those sons will never be. The fathers' seed is lost forever.

Where, as in the case of John and Robert Kennedy, sons were born, we do not know how they will be affected by the violent deaths of their fathers. Fear and resentment may keep them from following the Kennedy tradition of courage, excellence, the will to win. With only wealth and social position left, it is doubtful that the family can continue its present unity. Like the Kung family, like the Bouvier family, it may fall into separate parts, each pursuing its individual interest, indifferent to anything more, until the family disappears into the general mass and is no more.

On the other hand, there is the possibility that, given the right genes, there may emerge a few, or even one, who will be inspired by their martyred uncles and will rise to make their place in time and history. But they must be given time in which to grow and mature. It is their right. The absence of the father in this third generation will have an effect.

Edward Kennedy's youth, his own immaturity and indecision, compel the father image to be faint indeed. The Kennedy women, now robbed of these men upon whom they depended, remain as the outstanding symbols of strength for a third generation of Kennedys.

If Edward Kennedy retires, he may have time and energy to assume family leadership and build a father image strong enough to influence the younger generation. But then, the very fact of retirement may weaken the image. How shall courage be defined now?

Joan and Ted had wanted a large family. "Larger than Bobby's," they once said. Joan had two miscarriages, and it seemed, for a time, that she would not be able to bear any more children other than Kara and Teddy.

She has a special and quite rare problem. Happily, she carried Patrick to term, after obstetricians had taken every possible precaution to counteract her problem.

Ted had hoped for at least ten children. But there is little possibility for more now. Rose confided that she would be pleased if Teddy limited his family. "If Bob had listened to me," she said, "they would have stopped at eight or nine."

In early fall we read the sad news that Joan Kennedy had lost her most recently conceived baby. Inevitably Ted Kennedy will ask himself if the consequences of the unfortunate Cape Cod accident so distressed his wife that she was affected physically. The medical answer is probably no. The body has its own functions to perform. Other women who have been under mental strain have nevertheless produced healthy infants. But body and mind in a sensitive overwrought woman are closely connected. Mind does affect body and body does affect mind. There is no answer for the young husband. He must add this last catastrophe to the others that have preceded it.

At this point let us consider Joan Kennedy. We see her now and again but still vaguely. She lived for years in the shadow of Jacqueline Onassis and was only recently emerging from the shadow of Ethel Kennedy.

Her name is Virginia Joan Bennett and she lived with her family in Bronxville, New York, a girl so beautiful and blonde that when she was married in 1958 by Francis Cardinal Spellman to young Ted Kennedy, the *New York Daily News* gave its whole front page to her picture as she left St. Joseph's Church, in Bronxville, with her husband. Ted Kennedy was then studying law at the Univer-

sity of Virginia, and the young couple had a happy
year there together as he finished his course and
before he plunged into the family political fray.

She is a quiet young woman, a pianist so talented that she has been suggested as a guest artist
to benefit the Boston Symphony Orchestra. Beautiful as she is, people forget that she is also intelligent
and, to a degree, studious. During her husband's
last year at the university, she took courses in
sociology and American history.

Like the other Kennedy daughters-in-law, she
is a loyal and devoted member, and equally as devoted a mother and wife. Her first purpose in life
has been to make and keep husband and children
happy and the home pleasant and a good place in
which to rest, play, and grow.

Her children go to Beauvoir School and she is
faithful in her attendance at all school functions. No
television at home, by the way, on school nights,
and this rule is upheld by both parents.

Like all the Kennedy women, Joan Kennedy is
deeply religious, and a Roman Catholic. Religious
duties, home duties, her membership on the board
of Washington's National Symphony Orchestra,
her obligations as the wife of a young senator keep
her busy. People like her. She takes time to talk to
people when she is campaigning with her husband.
She does not enjoy the campaigns. She says, "If I
weren't married to Ted, I'd be home with my
children leading a much more private life. I really

don't enjoy doing this kind of thing. I do it because I love Ted.''

A very rich soul, a friend describes her, and an honest one, it may be added. She has, on occasion, criticized even her husband, urging him to be more human in his approach to people, and to put his thoughts into language they can understand easily. In some ways — endearing, everyday ways — she is like her sister-in-law Ethel. But Ethel makes friends more easily, is more frolicking, more lively, less reserved.

My impression of Joan is that she does not wish to be conspicuous. When she wore a miniskirt at a White House dinner, it was not to defy request or convention. The set hour was early, six o'clock, dress was not specified, and others as well as she took the occasion to be semiformal. Whatever her qualities, and they are genuinely good and in some ways unusual, the important fact is that by her marriage she willingly and wholeheartedly became a Kennedy, more perhaps than her sister-in-law Ethel has been able to do.

If Ethel does not marry again, the Kennedy stamp upon her will be permanent. If she does marry again, it will not, and so strong is her personality, so keyed to the man in the house, that she will develop in new ways as has Jacqueline Onassis — or perhaps, to be more precise, her own true personality will define itself. The Kennedy strength deeply influenced the woman each Kennedy married. In addition, there has been the influence of the unified family. Jacqueline has escaped from it. Is it possible that Ethel will do so? Will Joan? Today's newspapers, on my desk before me, carry the report that Joan will divorce her husband. It is one of the thirty-six ways of escape.

An old Chinese proverb says, "Of the thirty-six ways of escape, the best is to run away." Perhaps this is true. I cannot say. But in the lives of most women — why do I not speak the whole truth? — in the life of every woman there may come a moment which she recognizes. It is the moment when she decides that she can endure no more. Then she must determine her escape.

Each Kennedy woman, born or married, has faced that moment. It is an inevitable moment, the Kennedy men being what they are — handsome, volatile, impetuous, brilliant, and susceptible to women. In a word, they are incurably Irish. It will take generations of other breeding to get the Irish diluted enough to make it "safe" for any woman to marry a Kennedy man. One generation is not enough.

———·◆●◆·———

Put women aside, and in the Kennedy family they have always been aside waiting until needed, the real decision of the family's future lies within Edward Kennedy. He is the last adult male in a family of noteworthy men, and it is not clear whether he can match their greatness. Perhaps he is not sure that he wants to.

Greatness demands a heavy price in self-sacrifice and self-discipline. Moreover, ours is not an age of great men. Once upon a time history was made by unique men, and when it was written down it was the story of exceptional men and what they did. Now history is made up of events shaped not by strong and powerful personalities but by haphazard effects, one upon another.

The full danger of the human situation can only be comprehended when one realizes that ours is a time of giant events and grave issues, but not of great men. Even women have ceased to progress toward an increased sense of responsibility, as citizens tend instead to retreat into the small, safe areas of domesticity.

As I write a delivery of new magazines and newspapers arrives at my desk. Every one of them carries a headline regarding Ted Kennedy. There is a pursuit of his every movement that is almost ghoulish.

This is in direct opposition to the principles of fair trial as drawn up by attorneys recently, which are that accused persons are presumed innocent until proved guilty. They are entitled also to be judged in an atmosphere free from passion, prejudice, and sensationalism. The relentless reporting that seems to pursue the Kennedy men and women creates an atmosphere in which it is all but impossible to discover persons free from prejudice who could serve as jurors in case of any trial. No one's reputation should be needlessly injured, but the reputation of the Kennedy family has certainly been so injured again and again.

———·••·———

I first met Senator Edward Kennedy on a warm spring day when I went upon appointment to his office in Washington. I had a purpose, not political. I wanted to ask his permission to use certain material in a piece of writing I had engaged to do. I was promptly on time, but when I entered I was told that, although the senator had not yet returned from luncheon, he would be in shortly.

I am always interested in men's offices. They are as revealing as are the houses that women tend. John Kennedy's office had been comfortably and handsomely informal. Robert Kennedy's office had been severely furnished and was orderly and somewhat bare. Edward Moore Kennedy's office was crowded and disorderly and busy with hurrying young girls and a few young men. Books and papers were piled on the floor, bookshelves were jammed, telephones were ringing incessantly. The atmosphere was one of haste and busyness, if not of confusion.

I am not good at waiting and I felt impatience

growing within me. I had come some distance to keep this appointment, and I had another appointment pending. At last my patience ended abruptly. I rose. Immediately, a charming young girl called to me that the senator was expecting me now. I relented and went into his office.

A tall, rather heavyset young man rose to meet me, telephone in hand, for he was talking to someone, but we shook hands and I sat down. His telephone conversation went on, and I took the opportunity to study this young man. Taller than his brothers, I thought, but not as slim or as clean-cut as the two I had known. He looks more like his mother, perhaps, face rounder than his brothers' faces, a bit jowlish, the complexion not quite so clear, the eyes smaller, but a handsome face notwithstanding, and nothing wrong that hard exercise and controlled eating and drinking could not improve.

He did not have his brothers' immaculate grooming, either. His suit could have done with a pressing, and he wore it with an informality almost boyish. He began talking as soon as he put down the receiver, telling me how busy he was, and what his next appointment was and how important. His brothers, more sophisticated, had instead lent themselves immediately to me and had showed an interest in my purpose in coming to see them, which, genuine or not, marked them as perhaps more experienced than this young senator.

But I liked him, nevertheless, and was interested in what he had to say and in observing, while he talked, the signs I recognized so well from my experience with my own three sons, the importance of the position in any family of each son. Edward Kennedy showed signs of a boy who had been born the youngest son. There was a certain strain in him, the result, doubtless, of having to compete with older and perhaps more brilliant brothers, a handicap which I discussed earlier.

These were my thoughts as I sat listening to the young senator and watching his face. I broke in at last to make my errand known. He scarcely paused to listen, another difference between him and his brothers. They were older, more secure in themselves, finding it less necessary to prove the importance of what they were doing.

The ability to listen to another person's conversation, interests, points of view, is a sign of maturity, when position is beyond question. The youngest child in a family has to chatter, argue, clamor, insist, demand, and if necessary perform a tantrum to define his position.

I have a five-year-old grandson, a miracle of brilliance and mischief, who, when his father, in a state of uncontrollable exasperation, lifts the paddle to administer justified punishment, holds up his microscopic right hand and in the pontifical manner of a seasoned lawyer says, "Now wait a minute, dad. Let me first explain exactly why — " and he explains *ad infinitum* until he establishes his position.

This same small boy in the midst of the large family circle manages by sheer continuing conversation to monopolize the entire attention of the assembly and gain, thereby, the sympathy of every member. Such are the attributes of youngest sons, and by these means they escape the disciplines and standards which have impelled the older sons.

I never knew a youngest son, for example, who was not a reckless driver. My own youngest son, now a thoroughly stable citizen, was at a period of his life a wild man behind the wheel. Indeed, when he was at Harvard, his marks suffered from his obsession with racing cars. I have been inclined, therefore, to understand the young senator's propensity to fast driving. Breaking speed laws is a sign of insecurity of some sort, the need to prove one's self. When maturity develops, the need no longer exists, and the speedometer drops back to normal.

The question may be asked, how long does this last? The answer is that the length of time varies with the individual. In Edward Kennedy's case, it may last longer than it might otherwise have done, since he had three older brothers of extraordinary brilliance and ability. Even his sisters have the Kennedy force and charm. The competition has been severe.

In his office I admired a hand-carved desk,

rather small. It has a leather top and in one corner there is a plaque which says, "For Joseph P. Kennedy III." There are also these initials, "J.B.K." The initials stand for Jacqueline Bouvier Kennedy. The desk belonged to Joseph Kennedy, Jr., the eldest son of the family. The plaque is for the eldest son of Robert Kennedy. Robert Kennedy himself used the desk. Now Edward has it, but some day it will go to young Joe III.

On the wall of this office there is also a framed report card, all As except one C. It belonged once to Rose Kennedy and was discovered, Edward Kennedy told me, by his brother Jack, who, adjured by his parents to get better grades in school, retaliated by discovering an old report card of his mother's. She, a straight A student as a rule, but now with a C? On Jack's quipping letter she had written a few words to the effect that he should do what she said, not what she did.

My visit with Edward Kennedy that day ended on a strongly affectionate family note. We spoke of his mother, and it was apparent that he is extremely proud of her. Family feeling was strong and extended warmly to the children, nephews, and nieces.

As I left, I wondered: Will this man ever become president?

12

WE HAVE espoused the principles of democracy, we live according to its laws and ideals. All might be well in such an idealistic system were it not for the fact, not sufficiently realized, that a democracy is essentially competitive. Everyone has an equal chance, at least theoretically, to succeed. Theoretically each one is as good as any other one and has the same right to try, the same opportunity to try, to become rich and powerful.

The hitch is that in the inevitable competition some are more successful than others because of the congenital qualities of talent and will. These are the natural winners. In our generation in the United States, the Kennedy men have been natural winners. They have had the combination of wealth, good looks, high spirit, natural talent, and resolute determination.

Such an abundance of blessings can lead only to trouble and ultimately, as we have witnessed, even to death. Our people simply cannot tolerate so stunning a combination. Upon one pretext or another, such persons who "have everything" must be eliminated. Fredric Wertham, the well-known psychiatrist, calls it "magnicide, the killing of somebody big." Democracy, says David Riesman, Harvard sociologist, presents the question, "Why are you so big and why am I so small?"

This weakness in our competitive system cannot be cured by repressive police measures. These in themselves would deny the very bases of the democratic system. The Kennedy family presents the perfect example of the monstrous crime which denies democracy itself. The violence of mass and individual envy of the talented and successful person may even prevent such persons from fulfilling themselves.

Yet we desperately need talented persons. They are the leaders so necessary to benefit the mass. We need them at every level of life. In my own small way, for example, I have shared in the experience that has all but destroyed the Kennedys.

It was in college that I realized how dangerous it was to be popular, how dangerous it was to succeed. I had grown up in the family-sheltered, non-competitive Chinese society where, if I did my best, I received only respect and praise. Not so in my own society! I was first sharply impressed by this fact when in my senior year at college, needing the prize money for graduation expenses, I entered the short-story contest and the poetry contest. Unfortunately for my popularity, I won both. Instead of eager, friendly faces, I met hostile looks and mutters that it was not "fair" to give two prizes to one person.

Years later when I received the Nobel Prize for Literature, totally unexpected, there was a wave of anger that a woman, and a woman who had spent most of her life in China, should be given the award as an American.

Robert Frost, bless him, said, "If *she* can get the Nobel Prize, anyone can"; Theodore Dreiser, who was a faithful correspondent of mine, abruptly ceased writing; Henry Canby, then editor of the *Saturday Review of Literature,* wrote an excoriating editorial; and so on, *ad infinitum.* The rancor still exists in certain circles, but I have learned to understand it. In our country the greatest crime, in the popular mind, is to fail. The American cannot forgive himself and, therefore, he will not forgive others who have been successful when he has failed.

Where the provocation has been extreme, as in the case of the Kennedys, the result has been fatal and, in my opinion, will be again, and even again. Certain of the Kennedy grandsons show signs of the strong Kennedy combination of charm, ambition, and will. The tragedy of this generation may pursue them into the next. The Kennedys know this and fear haunts them.

Few men are strong enough, however talented,

to live their lives under such conditions and few women are brave enough to be their wives. Yet, until now, the Kennedy men have been strong enough and the Kennedy women brave enough, and in justice they deserve all honor, although they will not get it, for in situations involving the emotions one must not expect justice.

Yes, the Kennedy women are haunted by fear. They must accept fear as an inescapable part of their lives. Again, it is to their credit that they are faithful to their men and do not try to change them, knowing doubtless that such men not only must not be changed but cannot be changed. Their destiny is shaped by what they are, and if a woman is not able to learn how to live with fear, she must leave the man whose life is lived in the midst of fear. It is a tribute to the women who have loved and stayed married to Kennedy men that none of them has left her husband. Of the Kennedy women who have married other men, two have stayed married because their husbands were strong enough to merge their lives with the interests and concerns of their powerful family, and this with notable individual responsibility and contribution.

I do not mean to give the impression that the Kennedy women have been crippled by fear. Quite the opposite is true. In the midst of fear, they live fearlessly. I suppose that religion tempers women more than it does men, especially, again perhaps, the Roman Catholic faith. But a woman who marries a man like the Kennedy men must have endless patience and capacity for unselfish, bottomless love.

These daring, impetuous, brilliant men live at a height and tensity unknown to the average man. They are in constant competition not only with other men but with themselves. Today's achievement is not good enough for tomorrow. They must constantly excel their own records. A high mountain is not high enough. They are not satisfied until they have climbed the highest and face the empty sky.

To sail a boat upon calm waters is not enough. They must risk their lives to shoot the most dangerous rapids. Remind them that there are other lives than their own to consider and the reminder only makes the challenge greater because the risk is greater. They take every gamble, win or lose. Three Kennedy sons have lost. The future of the fourth is darkly shadowed by doubts.

The endless patience of Kennedy wives, their bottomless capacity for love have been tried most sorely, however, not only by the crises of daring and the recklessness of instinctive courage, but as well by the need for ready acceptance of the unexpected events of any day. For the high mood in which such men live rises inevitably to acts of unbelievable folly. Tension finds relief in wild gaiety, in reckless behavior, more fitting to adolescents than to great men.

Lesser folk may marvel at the seemingly inexplicable contrast between inspired wisdom and almost childish pranks when tension relaxes, and relax it must, for nature demands reaction after action. A calm, reflective temperament does not produce such extremes, but also does not reach such heights of power and daring. A nation may be shocked to read of revels so childish that guests are pushed fully clothed into swimming pools, and drunkenness is acceptable.

We should not be shocked, however. These men upon whom the challenge of life lies heaviest must escape sometimes into a child's world again, a refuge where they can escape the daily demands of leadership and behave as children do, laugh as children laugh, throw caution aside, forget for the moment who they are and are doomed to be, and must be because they are born to leadership.

The women who marry the Kennedy type of man understand this. They do not feel they need to forgive anything, for to them there is nothing to forgive. They love their men exactly as they are. They want their men to be and do what the men themselves wish to be and do.

"She's a great supporter for a husband," Robert Kennedy said of his wife, Ethel, after eighteen years of marriage. "She always thinks I'm right and they're wrong."

When he was debating with the Kennedy family whether he should run for the presidential candidacy, his wife, knowing, doubtless, that his real desire was to do so, upheld him against all objections. Moreover, she insisted that the decision was his alone. She said:

"That shows you how great Bobby is. He heard all the arguments and did what he thought was right."

Did she have bitter regrets when the tragedy of his assassination fell upon her and all the world? My guess is that she did not. Had he been persuadable, he would not have been the man she loved. He had fulfilled his own destiny.

Yet, as I ponder this relationship of man and woman, I wonder if it is not more easy — if easy is the word, since nothing between men and women is really easy — I wonder, I say, if it is not more easy to accept a single tragic event, even death, than it is to accept the smaller but not less difficult events of daily life, the constant uncertainty of set hours or promised engagements, always liable to change or cancellation, for example, to speak of small events, or, to move to deeper matters, to face the inevitable fact that the man who charms her into adoring love charms other women, too, and women today do not hesitate to pursue a man who charms them and may even make a profession of such pursuit.

And these men of heroic size, absorbed in the mighty deeds they conceive and perform, can be amazingly susceptible to such pursuit. Faithful in heart though they usually are to the essential women who are their wives, the need for the diver-

sion of play is very real. They are not so much
tempted by the other women as they are flattered,
amused, and easily aroused sexually. It is part of
the necessity to escape, though only for a short time,
for actually they live the life they want to live, a
life of constant challenge and achievement, without
which they would be desperate with boredom.

Again the wife must understand the need and
in silence accept the temporary diversion and hold
her place steady until her man returns to his life
again, which is his work.

It is not only the wife upon whom the shadow
of a great man falls. There are also the children.
Which of the Kennedy children will survive and
which will not? When I say survive, I do not mean
death. They are a healthy group, they live in ideal
physical conditions with plenty of outdoors and
good food and good schools and loving family life.
I mean survive as individuals in the aura of family
fame and greatness.

I think of a man I know, a man like the Kennedy
men, a driving, talented, successful man who has
built his own empire in business. With every ambition fulfilled and every desire satisfied, apparently
he has everything.

Yet his wife, a beautiful woman to see, is a
hopeless alcoholic. His son has all his father's

charm and good looks — and is a weakling, failing in college, involved already in a scandal with a girl, a bitter disappointment to his father who coldly and silently gets him out of one scrape and another.

The husband is too powerful for the wife, the father is too successful for the son. Simply by being what he was born to be, this man has no personal satisfaction in his family. Everyone knows he has a mistress. His wife and his son know, too, and, aware of their own failure, they sink still lower in their own self-esteem — which he understands, moreover, but cannot help. He, too, can only be what he was born to be, a leader, a ruler, a maker in the modern world.

I have known not a few men who were sons of great fathers and none of these sons have been great men. At best they have been good men in a quiet way, but more often they are failures even as men. Some of them are apologetic and speak of their fathers with affectionate respect. Some hate their fathers because they hate themselves, knowing how they have failed themselves and their fathers.

And the fathers know how the shadow of their own success and greatness has fallen upon their children. I speak with feeling on this subject, for I have my own experience, though in my own small way.

"It is hard to be your child," my own children have told me. "The least little thing we do wrong, even if it's only driving a few miles over the speed limit, and everyone in the neighborhood gossips about it.''

I know they often feel restricted because they are my children, although I myself do not restrict them. When they were still in school, I remember, I made a close inspection of them before they went to school in the morning or anywhere, in fact, for if a button was missing or a sock not whole they would be pitied from one person to another for being the children of a mother who neglected them because she was a writer, or because she was somewhere in Europe or Asia, or because she left them with servants, or any number of reasons.

The children were always on show, so to speak, and they knew it and I knew it and more than once apologized to them for the inconvenience of being my children. Such apologies they received with the utmost courtesy, assuring me politely that they did not mind it excessively, and informing me for my own comfort that if it became unbearable they would invite a fight, which indeed they sometimes did. Then I was the one to receive a telephone call, very irate, to tell me that one of my sons had made another woman's son have a nosebleed.

"I am surprised that one of *your* children —" she always said.

"Don't be surprised," I always broke in, "you can't imagine how awful it is to be a child of mine."

My sympathies are of course divided between the generations. I understand so well how merely being one's self and fulfilling one's own destiny, whatever it may be, can bring results upon the dearly loved children, and how the children can and indeed must suffer, inescapably, for what their parents achieve.

In the Kennedy family the suffering is the heavier, I think, because the achievement was so extraordinary. I also firmly believe the greatest tragedy of the Kennedy family, the one which has weighed heaviest upon the women because they could do nothing to prevent it or alleviate it, has been the cruelty of the crowd. Joseph Patrick Kennedy, the father, knew well this supreme cruelty, and toughened his sons for the political battle.

In his son John's first political campaign in Boston, John Kennedy had his own experience. A woman of the opposing party attacked him with accusations, and though she had whispered to him at the door, "Don't pay any attention — it's just politics," he did pay attention and attacked her in return. Perhaps this prepared him for the price of his winning even his first political nomination.

He was only twenty-nine years old at the time and friends of his defeated opponents declared that his father had masterminded the election, had poured millions into radio and newspaper advertising, had tried to split the Italian vote. Of course, the father had helped the son, but no amount of manipulation could have won a ten-man primary race.

John Kennedy had won fairly, but the lying innuendos in this first campaign began the rising jealousy of men which ended finally in his assassination. The women of the family could not fight back in any way whatsoever.

Women cannot fight back as men can, openly and with all the weapons at command. They can only retreat or, at best, accept what takes place in life. As a consequence, the inner rebellion deepens and in depth becomes a dominating power in their lives. So it is, I believe, with the Kennedy women today.

Rose Kennedy, for example, is stronger than ever in her faith that God works and will work for the good of her family. If she is like most grandmothers, her faith is now for her grandchildren and in her grandchildren. What perhaps she does not realize is that her grandchildren are living in an entirely new era. Times have not only changed but have changed rapidly.

Her grandchildren do not resemble their parents, her own children. The second-generation Kennedys were not only under the severe but loving domination of their father, Joseph Patrick Kennedy, aided by his faithful wife, their mother, but they were born into an era when the patterns of life were clear, especially for the rich.

There was very little latitude in their environment, but there is also only slight evidence that they demanded latitude. What small effort there was in that direction was made only by the youngest son,

Edward, and to that extent he has been and is a bridge between his parents' era and that of the third Kennedy generation, the grandchildren.

The grandchildren belong to the new age, the age of youth. For it is a truism that ours is an age dominated by youth — or at least by people under twenty-five.

Young people complain that older people dominate them, that older people have created this unsatisfactory world, that they have grown up helplessly in the rigid environment of an Establishment against which they rebel. The truth is that the environment of which they so bitterly complain *has been shaped by them.*

Their parents, the adults, were and are responsible only for creating an environment that they fondly believed was what the children wanted. Our entire culture ever since the end of World War II has been designed for the young. Even the garments we wear, the styles in which they are cut, are suited mainly for the young. A middle-aged figure, male or female, looks absurd in a miniskirt designed for the slim, flat-chested shape of a teen-age girl, or jaunty, hip-hugging slacks made for a boy under twenty.

Or, to turn to other fields.

Must television programs and plays and even books take it for granted that our country is dominated solely by the wishes of children and adolescents? I can only reply by saying yes, it must be taken for granted because it is true.

It is time for us, the parents and adults, to consider what we have done. With the best will possible, wanting only to do what is right for the children, we have created a world against which they now rebel. Stupid youth? Or stupid parents? Both.

Adults since the end of World War II have been baby-tenders instead of strong individuals deciding for themselves what should be their own contribution to their times. Men have worked day after dull day to do no more than breed, feed, and clothe a gaggle of children. Women have been servants their lives long to these same children.

Now these children are old enough, the boys to grow beards, the girls to produce babies out of wedlock, to turn on their parents and accuse them. Accuse them of what? Basically, to accuse them of not having had time enough to do more than feed and clothe them, pay their school taxes and dentists' bills, They are oblivious to the fact that there *was* no more time.

It takes not only time but leisure for the creative spirit to reflect and ruminate and in such mood to devise the stimulating brilliance of new ideas and acton. Busy with breeding children to replace the losses of two world wars, two generations of Americans have devoted themselves to the swarms of young who now threaten our culture, even our civilization, with their destructive rebellious demand for that which they themselves have prevented.

In fairness, I must remind myself that people

are usually at the mercy of blind natural impulses, seeking always to replace what has been lost. In the same fairness I must remind myself that the young did not ask to be born. Both generations have been used by blind old Mother Nature. Now we face one another, dismayed and helpless, unless we understand what has happened and that, but only by cooperation, we can build a better world for all.

The question is, how can we remedy what is already past? Brilliant men have spent their lives in making money for the children they have begotten, and intelligent, able women have lost years in being cooks and chauffeurs. The young cannot help their elders for they do not know how to do so, and the elders can only look back over the inevitable years, the only result of which is the complaining, domineering young who are bewildering as well as bewildered.

So much for the kind of world the young Kennedys face today! What, I wonder, will they do? They have the advantage — or the disadvantage — of great wealth. They will not have to struggle and compete merely to make a living. But will they have the ability to "cope" with their heritage that, to their grandmother, is a secret to successful living?

"Teddy will cope," she said confidently after the death at Chappaquiddick. For weeks his inability to pull himself out of depression belied his mother's prediction. He was understandably withdrawn, low-keyed, pensive. He felt that his career had been terminally damaged.

Then, slowly, in time, he regained his spirit. "It will all come out," he said one day. "The questions. All the answers. It will all come out, and I think people will understand. Nineteen seventy? In Massachusetts? Yes, I'll run."

Will the people "understand"? I am not so sure. I believe that, at this point, our people are angry with Kennedys even while they love them. I use the Kennedy name symbolically, although the Kennedy family more than any other in the United States is a symbol of the American dream. From rags to riches in three generations *is* the American Dream, but, being idealists and the children of idealists, we think of riches as more than money. Riches include heroic qualities of character and, more remotely, of culture.

The Kennedys had all of this, or very nearly. Among the "beautiful people" they were perhaps the most "beautiful." Their spectacular success at being "beautiful" roused unbearable dissatisfaction in spectacularly unsuccessful persons and assassinations provided the only outlet.

People were secretly satisfied and yet truly remorseful at the same time. They were triumphant though ashamed. Conflicting emotions? Of course! We Americans are shot through with conflicting emotions.

The Kennedy Women

Democracy breeds conflicting emotions because it encourages freedom. It also demands individual responsibility. A totalitarian state is simple enough. One is either for or against it; there is no freedom or individual responsibility and, consequently, no confusion of emotions.

The greatest conflict of all is that we destroy our heroes. We demand heroes. We need heroes. We create them.

A movie star, a sportsman, let anyone rise above the average of his kind, and we acclaim him and compel him to be a hero, a national figure. When he rises too high above us, however, we destroy him by murder or by scorn or by false accusation. Then we search for and create another hero.

Thus having destroyed two Kennedy brothers, we fastened our eager gaze upon the last brother. We were in the usual process of building him into a national idol when he committed the unforgivable sin of failing us as a new god. He behaved as an ordinary man behaves, or would like to behave.

He, a married man, went to a party where the girls were all unmarried. Worst of all, he behaved so stupidly that the escapade became known through an incredible unexplained tragedy.

How could a hero, a candidate for an idol, so betray us? Your would-be idolators will never "understand" this, Senator, I assure you.

It is terrifying to become a hero in a democracy! No man or woman in his right senses could wish for great success. For when such persons rise above the success of others, they can never again live in peace and safety.

Long before that last blow, there are obscene and threatening telephone calls, filthy and angry anonymous letters, and the long procession of fawning false friends, until in the end one learns to live in solitude and loneliness. But even that guarantees no peace.

The press, radio, and television hunger to feed the people the scandals they crave in their desire to destroy the famous, the successful, the outstanding, whom they both hate and love. The media of communication search for evil news about the gods and goddesses, our national heroes and heroines, and if they find nothing they create "news" out of rumor and lies. And our people believe them.

Only yesterday I saw in a California daily newspaper so foul a lie about Jacqueline Onassis that I was glad she had married a man who is the citizen of another country. I hope she never sees that newspaper, for if she does she can only be wounded to the heart, as Edward Kennedy has been. And his gentle wife, his lovely children, all his family will have no more redress than if they were thrown to wolves. No one can save them or even help them. A few good people may wish to help, but they are afraid to do so. Prudence keeps them silent and injustice prevails.

Something has gone wrong in our country. The Kennedy family should by now have achieved a certain trust, an understanding. Instead the third generation, the grandchildren of Joseph Patrick Kennedy and Rose Kennedy, face a distraught future, in which the odds are against them.

If I were a Kennedy mother, I would take my children far away to another land and among another people, let them grow up in peace and ignorance of the past. What is it the wise old Book says?

"The fathers have eaten sour grapes and the children's teeth are set on edge."

Yes, I would take the children far away from the haunted past. I would take them to some old country where the people, wise in ancient culture, know how to accept each person as he is, respecting talent, valuing beauty, granting time for mind and spirit to develop.

Here in the United States we have not had time to develop a culture of our own. Our passion for equal rights has blinded us to the fact that Nature herself does not grant equal rights. Some of us are beautiful and some are not. Some of us are talented and some are not. Some of us are brilliant and some are not.

While grace, beauty, and talent do not result from riches alone, where these treasures exist wealth fosters them more freely than poverty, and wealth has its values thereby in cultured terms. Culture has not been endemic in our society.

Pioneers are not usually cultured men, and, consequently, not understanding their own lack, they sneer at culture in others. Are we not past the pioneer stage? Actually we are not. We are bored if not downright embarrassed in the presence of brilliant people. Our envy verges on hostility and even fear. We prefer the mediocre. I hear cries:

"But we are the most generous —"

Stop there, please! We are generous. But I remember the retort that a friend of mine, a man who belongs to a small Asian country, made to me when I myself reminded him of our generosity.

"You are generous," he agreed. "But not with yourselves. Only with your money."

It takes time to develop generosity over and above money. It takes a certain quality of life. We are too young, I believe, to have developed quality.

It takes time — time — time — to understand the subtleties of individual human nature, and in our general atmosphere of cultural mediocrity, though superb technology, it may be too much to expect understanding of our small but highly talented aristocracy.

We still apply to the valuable few the merciless restrictions of our Puritanic past. We expect of our talented minority behavior even stricter, morally speaking, than we expect of the mediocre majority.

In short, we do not value talent except as a financial commodity. We fail to recognize that without the talented minority, the mediocre majority can make no progress.

Only time will tell whether a Kennedy personality, forceful as it is, can withstand the destructive and battering forces of democracy. For every positive has its negative. The positive force of democracy lies in its philosophy of equal opportunity for every individual to develop to his fullest capacity. Democracy, however, does not promise equal benefits to all. It merely guarantees opportunity. But ignorant and unthinking persons confuse these rights, and gradually there has developed an unrealistic attitude toward life which assumes that the fruits of life are also to be divided equally, regardless of the individual's ability to achieve these fruits. The result of such an unrealistic attitude is the development of a sullen mood among the less fortunate segments of our society, and even an arrogant conviction that one person is as "good" as another. This results finally in a real hostility on the part of people of inferior minds and talents against the talented and successful. So severe is the hostility that it results in character assassination at best and actual murder at worst.

The danger of this hostility is emphasized when the success of an individual has been spectacularly swift, as in the case of the Kennedy family. Rose Kennedy herself recently expressed this danger when she speculated about the violence that has hounded her family. She wondered whether it was because "God doesn't permit" the kind of success the Kennedys have achieved in their swift rise from humble origin. "Sometimes I wonder," she mused, "if there is something about my family that invites violence. Is it envy?" And as she said later in regard to the marriage of Jacqueline Kennedy, "We Kennedys never do things in just ordinary fashion; it's always a big explosion."

What makes the Kennedys not "ordinary" is, of course, their sense of style, their flair, their independence. Secure in their family unity, confident of their own ability, they have never felt threatened by society. They still refuse to be threatened.

"None of us is especially pietistic or solemn about religion," Eunice Shriver says, "but mother has a burning faith similar to that of the great martyrs who would rather die for their faith than live without it. It came, I think, from her Irish heritage."

"I am not going to be vanquished by these events," Rose Kennedy declares. "I don't intend to be laid low or pulverized. If I collapsed, the morale of the whole family would be lowered."

"We have known joy and sorrow," Mrs. Kennedy said a few days before the death of her husband, Joseph, the Kennedy patriarch. "The agony and the ecstasy. And I must be grateful, because our triumphs have been greater than our tragedies."

An absolute faith in God can have its repercussions and its opposing effects. I speak from my experience with my dear missionary father. He had the burning faith of which Eunice Shriver speaks. He sought God's will and always found it. Once having found it, he clung to it without a moment's doubt. He did not recognize the possibility that God's will seemed frequently, too frequently, in fact, to coincide with his own desires, and his insistence upon a direct line to God roused in his fellow missionaries an opposition that at times amounted to fury. This he considered persecution, and he accepted it although at times he suffered real hardship, relentlessly, nevertheless.

I do not mean to suggest the possibility of the same confusion in Rose Kennedy. I do know, however, that relentless faith can produce a strength of character which may rouse opposition and invite retaliation. The mother's strong will can influence the children to develop a like strength, though it may be used for their own wishes, and thereby they arouse hatred from others not so strong, or, if as strong, then violently so.

Be this as it may, Rose Kennedy instilled strength into her children. She loves them passionately but with a controlled love. She has framed a heartbreaking poem, written by an Irish poet:

Lord, I do not grudge
My two sons that I have seen go out to break their strength and die, they and a few, in bloody protest for a glorious thing.

They shall be spoken of among their people. The generations shall remember them and call them blessed.

But I will speak their names to my own heart in the long nights, the little names that were familiar once around my dead hearth.

Though I grudge them not, I weary, weary of the long sorrow.

And yet I have my joy.

They were faithful and they fought.

173

13

ALL THIS is by way of introduction to my defense of the Kennedys in America. Again I speak of the Kennedys symbolically, as the most spectacular of our handful of leading families. We are today working steadily to destroy them.

Take up any newspaper and you will find a new "scandal" about a Kennedy or at least the rehash of an old scandal.

Secretaries, nurses, servants, and others rush in to prove to us how evil, how heartless, how unpleasant the Kennedys are, and how impossible they were as employers. To all these I can only ask, "Then why did you continue to work for them at all?" Of course, no reply need be made. If there were no readers of such scandal, if there were no enjoyment of smut, none would be printed. That it is printed, and read, is a grave reflection on our average American public.

The Kennedy Women

I am not so naïve as to believe that the Kennedys are entirely guiltless. That would be unrealistic, also. I have known enough brilliant and talented persons to realize that they are subjected to monstrous temptations. I know very well the temptations to which the Kennedys have sometimes yielded.

Rose Kennedy showed for years a steadfast loyalty to her husband while he continued a long relationship with a beautiful film actress. Outwardly, she maintained a proud silence. But the inner struggle must have left its mark upon the children. Perhaps no word was ever spoken, yet none needed to be spoken. There is confusion bred into the minds of children when they love their parents, and want to win their approval, and yet perceive a contradiction that prevents their own entire approval of those parents.

The Kennedy men were never celebrated for faithfulness to their wives, but their wives found it worthwhile to continue as wives and mothers. Their religion enjoins them to such faithfulness. But I believe there is more than religion as a reason. The Kennedy men have a quality so unusual that they attract may women, including their wives.

Their wives eventually realize that this is inevitable. They know how severe are the temptations for any young, handsome man in our society. If, in addition to all else, he is wealthy, practically any woman is available to him.

"You have no idea how hard it is to avoid the

women," a young man said to me. "They offer themselves, they throw themselves at you. They maneuver —"

"So long as you know it," I suggested.

He grinned. "They are so damnably clever. You get caught *before* you know it."

What he did not say was that the talented, brilliant man or woman has deep, strong feelings. They are usually lonely and are, therefore, more susceptible than average people. They can be easily tempted — alas, they often yield. When they do yield, we must not condemn without due consideration of their total value. Since they have much to give to our national life, since they are irreplaceable because we do not know how to create them, it behooves us to weigh evil against good and not destroy them.

Let it not be thought that I am advocating a totally noncritical attitude on the part of the public toward our symbolical Kennedys. The Kennedys have a responsibility to the public, if they seek public life, to maintain acceptable standards of behavior. These standards are amazingly steadfast the world around. Justice, reliability, wisdom define a good man or woman anywhere in the world. And everywhere in the world people long for such persons whom they can trust. If I have emphasized the cruelty of the crowd toward the talented minority capable of becoming their leaders, I must also emphasize the responsibility of the talented minority to fulfill the nobility of talent.

For talent can be a quality apart from the person upon whom it is bestowed. Sometimes, alas, all too often, a glorious talent is given to a person of weak will and ignoble ideals. I will not mention living persons who could exemplify what I mean.

Let me mention, for example, Edgar Allan Poe, a man of brilliant imagination who never achieved the fulfillment of his talent because of drunkenness. The genes that are handed on to a newborn child may be accompanied by other genes which include weaknesses of character unworthy of such a talent.

I think of a woman, now dead, who possessed superb talent for sculpture but lacked the profundity of mind that could have inspired her imagination to great creative production. Lacking the imagination, she created technically perfect sculpture, but not sculpture of greatness.

I cannot tell whether John Fitzgerald Kennedy could have fulfilled his talents had he been allowed to live. The signs are that he could have, for his mind was developing rapidly toward bold and imaginative thinking, which, applied to world affairs and with the administrative powers of his high position, might have made him a world leader.

His brother, Robert Kennedy, had within him the promise of a greatness equally important, but in an area not so much intellectual as in his sensitivity to justice and human rights.

The promise of greatness is not yet evident to me in the third brother, Edward. He shows a lack of judgment, let us say, which is alarming in a potential leader. The people of any nation want to be able to rely upon the wisdom of their leaders and upon their honesty and practical sense. They have the right so to wish and so to demand. For a people can only progress as fast and as soundly as their leaders provide the leadership for them to do so. This leadership must be in three directions simultaneously if a nation is to be sound qualitatively and quantitatively.

Ideals are essential, but the procedure toward achieving those ideals must be possible and practical. They will limit progress if they are not. And the ideals must be such that they will inspire the people with confidence.

I should have to say that the Kennedys have failed in certain qualities of character. Granted, our people have often accused them falsely of foolish acts, some of them even immoral according to accepted standards of personal conduct in our country, granted all that I have said in previous pages, there has been an uneasiness among our people regarding the Kennedys which there was not in the case, say, of Coolidge, or of Hoover, or of Truman, to name only a few.

None of these men were as brilliant as the Kennedys, but people felt they were more trustworthy. Perhaps the so-called common people never quite trust the men and women more brilliant, more daring, more creative, than they themselves are. If this is true, then it behooves the brilliant, the daring, the creative, to prove to these others that they can and *will* be as trustworthy, as sensible, as wise, as the people long for them to be.

But — and here is the crux — if the education of the superior mind contains the learning of responsibility for the use of one's talents and abilities, then the chasm between the two extremes may be ended. If the less gifted can through experience learn to trust the most gifted, much of the present envy and jealousy and malice of the crowd toward the specially talented may change to gratitude that such minds and personalities exist as leaders.

———————

I see that in the course of this book I have covered a complete circle, from defense of the brilliant and talented minority, symbolized by the Kennedys, from which come all hopes for human progress, to defense of the majority who, dependent upon them for leadership, fear, distrust, and dislike them, while at the same time longing, unconsciously and inarticulately, for a leadership inspired by wisdom, justice, and a sense of responsibility.

Wherein have the Kennedys failed? Again I speak symbolically. I speak of a family that had more than wealth. The Rockefellers have had great wealth, and so have the Fords. Each family had a founding father comparable to Joseph Patrick Kennedy. Each family has produced a respectable second and third generation but no great popular leaders. Each family has been responsible for manifold good works of a humanitarian nature — witness the medical improvements of the Rockefeller Foundation, or the remarkable improvement in rice growing of the Ford Foundation, which, more than anything else, may solve the problem of starvation in India. These good works are not to be belittled but they are generic and have produced no leaders to inspire and encourage the soul of mankind.

John Fitzgerald Kennedy, before he was assassinated, was reaching that level of inspiration and, had he lived, he might have lifted us to a new understanding of our own national capacities and a true international leadership.

Under his influence, his wife might have continued her growth into a place of her own at his side. Without him, she has regressed into individualism and we hear only news of her new acquisitions in jewels, and her many possessions and amusements. The disappointment of the people who adored her, and were eager to see her grow into what they longed for her to be, is now expressed in bitter criticism and contempt that is really beyond what she deserves.

The same anger is turned upon Edward Kennedy, at whom people were beginning to look with hope, which in a single incident was dashed. Him also I doubt they can forgive. Even though they may, as he puts it, "understand," after all the questions are asked and answered I doubt that they will ever forgive.

I have just today received a letter from a grandson of the Kung family. He was a Red Guard leader in the very province in China where I grew up. I know every town and village of which he writes. He has just escaped to Taiwan, and from there he writes me that his grandmother, Madame Kung, who was my friend, had once hold him to write me when he could, and, when he wrote, to tell me the truth.

The truth he tells is of his own disillusionment. Among others like himself, the brilliant, the talented, the young, he was educated in a special school, designed for young men like himself. He was to be a leader. He was told, when he graduated, to go out among the people and teach them in turn. The people, he was told, were eager to learn. They were hopeful and happy. They lived simply but in far greater comfort than they had in the old days. He believed all he was taught, and he looked forward eagerly to undertaking his assignment.

When he went into the villages, however, he found that what he had been told was not true. The people were not happy. They were not well fed. They felt oppressed. He was overwhelmed by doubt and dismay. Being a Kung and in heart and brain still an aristocrat, he could not lie to them and he escaped. He went by foot to the southern coast, and found a fisherman's small junk that sailed to the islands as a smuggling vessel. Thus he escaped to Taiwan.

Rebel though he is, I was interested to perceive that his long indoctrination by communism made him critical, too, of what he saw in Taiwan. The people there, he wrote, were much richer and lived far more comfortably than they did on the mainland. But there were also far too many people who were really rich. They wore silk and satin garments, lived in big houses, and had many servants. This, he said, was wrong.

But he felt very confused, he said. There was, in fact, a great deal of freedom for everyone. Young men like himself, for example, could study what they wished in school. They could take up any profession they chose. They were not assigned as he had been assigned.

He had, for example, wished to become a writer, since his family had always been intellectuals. Instead, he had been trained as a teacher — in fact, a propagandist. But he could not bring himself to cheat his people. Now, perhaps, it was too late for him to become anything. Besides, what would he write? All he knew was communism in which he no longer could believe. And he was too old to go to school over again. He belonged nowhere. He was not happy anywhere.

On the other side of the world, under an entirely different system, I perceive the same tragic wastage of talent and brains that we have here — wasted because the possessors of the gifts, sorely needed by the world, are forced into a mold of criticism, arbitrary and destructive. They, as our young Americans, do not know what to believe.

———•—•—•———

The day Joseph Patrick Kennedy, Sr., died, the news was flashed around the world: another Kennedy death, but this time expected and therefore without horror. Only the death of the young is cruel. In course of time, at the end of a long and successful life, death is natural, death is good. How do I know? I know from my own experience.

When I was a child in China I saw death often, in wars and famines and unchecked disease, and always death was frightening and evil. Especially was it evil when the one dead was a child, a very young child.

We lived on a hill outside a great city, and the hillsides were covered with graves. Sometimes — too often — the graves were those of little children, and they were always shallow graves, the tiny bodies perhaps not even in coffins, or, if the family had been poor, not even clothed. Clothing was too valuable to be put into the ground to rot. The wild unfed dogs of the surrounding villages often found those small graves, and I, wandering child that I was, would sometimes come upon a tiny dead body, half-eaten, badly mauled. Then the full horror of death came over me and, sobbing aloud, all alone as I was, I would dig the hole deeper with my bare hands and gather the torn body, the severed parts, and bury them as best I could. So deeply did I feel death in those days, so fearful was its cruelty, that I could not speak of it to anyone, not even to my mother.

As the years passed, however, through the turmoil of wars and revolutions, I began to understand death better and to realize that there were times when death, inexplicable as it is and must ever remain, could be merciful and even welcome. And this I saw still later in my life when my own husband was stricken in exactly the same way that Joseph Patrick Kennedy was stricken, suddenly in the midst of health, on a summer's day, surrounded by his family. And I know the whole sad story, because I and my children lived it, too — the seeming recovery that after a period of treatment and rest almost made the man himself once more, but only almost and never quite the same. None of the family was ever quite the same, because there was the certain knowledge, the medical forewarning, that the blow would fall again and again until the last time. No day, no night, was secure from that knowledge, that certainty.

And so the blow did come, over and over, sometimes lightly, sometimes heavily, but always with destruction, until speech was gone, movement was lost, sight faded, the power of thought no more possible, and, most tragic of all, the ability to feel emotion, until before physical life actually ceased at the end of years the beloved man himself was gone. There in his chair he sat, day after day; moved to his bed at night, there he lay until day came again. His family surrounded him, but he was no longer the guiding force in their lives, he was no more the central power. And after that each member of the family must develop his own power, always based on the central force ingrained in him by the father.

So that last day came for Joseph Patrick Kennedy. The long process of dying ended in its natural and inevitable way, and in a way death is kind, for the process had been so gradual that when death came it was not even perceptible to the dying one. The capacity to feel had long ago ceased so there was no fear, no instant of panic. As I write these words, it is the night before the funeral. The body of Joseph Patrick Kennedy lies in its coffin in a comfortable room in his own home in Hyannis Port, from whence the big window looks out upon his favorite view over Nantucket Sound. Around him in the house his family is gathered in various places. I cannot know, but I do not doubt, that from time to time one or two, or several, enter the silent room and stand near him at that window, remembering what he has been as husband, as father, as grandfather. And, being a religious family, they will wonder if, or be sure, he is now somehow with his children on the other side of the invisible barrier, with young Joseph and Kathleen, with John Fitzgerald and Robert, and with John's little children who died almost before they lived. Children and grandchildren, they preceded him and hopefully, if one dares hope, they are there to welcome him. To Rose Kennedy, at least, and to Ethel Kennedy, there must be such thoughts. And perhaps, too, to Jacqueline Onassis, who in her own way loved Joseph Patrick Kennedy and was loved by him for the very independence which she above all his children, perhaps, possessed, and which he learned greatly to enjoy, once the initial shock of her difference was over and he understood her true and unique nature.

———•—•—•———

I write here in my Vermont home today and I think of them as I gaze across the room through the wide windows that open upon Stratton Mountain, where the children and grandchildren of Joseph Patrick Kennedy used often to come to ski on snowy days.

It was here that Robert Kennedy spent some time after those dangerous days when our President negotiated with Russia and a wavering Khrushchev following the Cuban missile crisis. It was necessary, perhaps, that he plunge into violent physical activity when he was in such a state of nervous tension as he endured during those days. He was of course always on call and could be reached at any instant, although he had given orders that he was only to be called on important matters. It was characteristic of him that though he could become impatient, even lose his temper, over small events, in times of crisis and danger he became fearless and cool.

Thus no one can really know the profound influence he had upon his brother, the President, nor the incalculable help he gave him, especially at that time of greatest danger, when all the world was threatened with final war, and two men, John Fitzgerald Kennedy and Nikita Khrushchev, each obligated to protect the interests of his nation, had also to consider the right and the necessity to protect the life of the human race.

At times of frightful danger men and women show their true selves. The weak and fearful dissolve into clamor and chaos. The strong and fearless become calm and resourceful. I speak of the Cuban missile crisis. The facts of that hour of supreme danger are few and simple. The year was 1962, the season was autumn, the day was October 16, at nine o'clock in the morning, when the President summoned his brother Robert to his office to tell him the intelligence division had studied a photograph just brought back from over Cuba by a U-2 on mission. It was apparent that Russia was bringing atomic weapons and missiles into Cuba. Later that same morning the Central Intelligence Agency reported to the highest officials of our government its conclusions, based on pictures and charts.

It is not necessary to repeat the well-known

events which followed. The significant fact is that the President chose in the days that followed to send his brother Robert again and again to meet with Ambassador Dobrynin to inform him of the President's concern. At these meetings, each of the utmost importance to the world, Robert Kennedy, though recognizing the obvious untruths of Dobrynin's assurances and denials, was able to maintain a calm firm insistence upon the truth.

In the end it was Robert Kennedy who advised that the United States should declare at once that we would not tolerate the Russian introduction into Cuba of missiles or other offensive weapons. The next day the President issued a warning, with full statement of what would happen if such events took place.

It is never possible for any president to be present at all consultative staff meetings. The very presence of an important personage inhibits full and free expression of opinions. This was especially true of President Kennedy, so dynamic and powerful was the effect of his controlled yet profound personality.

He did not, therefore, attend most of the decision-discussions, but instinctively these important men turned to Robert Kennedy for leadership. Those who were there have told of his firm, relentless, cool, and yet eminently just suggestions. Some men felt a military attack was necessary. Robert Kennedy, impetuous though he was, could also be prudent. He argued not for attack but for blockade and in the end this was the President's decision. For himself, Robert Kennedy simply said:

"I could not accept the idea that the United States would rain bombs on Cuba, killing thousands and thousands of civilians in a surprise attack."

It is significant of the Kennedy family, trained by such parents as Joseph Patrick and Rose Kennedy, that the moral aspects of any situation, however perilous, are nevertheless the most important. For five days of constant discussion of how to deal with the Cuban crisis, more time was spent on the moral effect of the surprise attack advocated by military advisers and even by such influential civilians as the brilliant Dean Acheson than on any other. It is not meaningless that one of Robert Kennedy's favorite quotations was from Keats's "The Fall of Hyperion":

> Who feel the giant agony of the world,
> And more, like slaves to poor humanity,
> Labor for mortal good . . .

The important fact in all that period of supreme peril of a third world war — and too few Americans realize how frightful was the danger — the two Kennedy brothers were successful in staving off that war. That they were capable of their decision, based first of all on what was right, is a tribute to the man who today is being consigned to his final home in the earth.

The Kennedy Women

Here in Vermont the rain is splashing against the wide windows of my mountain home. It is raining in Hyannis Port, too, the rain pounding on the roof of the parish church where a farewell service is being said for Joseph Patrick Kennedy. Around him are gathered his family, his wife, children, and grandchildren, the Kennedy clan, and a few close friends. Afterward he will be taken to the family burial ground in Holyhood Cemetery, in Brookline, nestled in the hills southwest of Boston. There may he rest in peace, for he leaves behind him a noble legacy in children and grandchildren, and may they never forget their memories of him, not only in the days of his fiery and powerful youth but in the days of his patient and dignified descent to death.

I am thinking now of the family. I am thinking especially of Rose Kennedy. It is the going home, the rain falling, the darkness deepening, the consciousness that the beloved person lies alone under the rain that make death intolerable. Her children are with her tonight but they too must leave her.

At last, alone, there comes to her the hour of realization. Carefully one performs the common rites of preparation for night, knowing that never again will anyone open her door, after she closes it. No voice will break the silence of her room. The bed is there and she lies down, knowing that never again will anyone share that bed. When she wakes, it will never again be to seek the comfort of the other presence.

Yes, he was ill for a long time and she is accus-

tomed to it but not to death and the awareness that
he lies forever in his grave. How well I know, how
well any woman knows who has experienced the
final separation of death! She does not see him now
as he has been in these recent years of age and illness; she will not see him as he lies in his grave
alone. Instead she remembers him as he was when
she married him, a tall, handsome young man, lean
and strong, his red hair and bright blue eyes — and
those dark-rimmed spectacles that made him look
as serious as a schoolteacher when all the time she
knew his impetuous ardent nature, his ready sense
of humor, his imperious will!

And then when the children came, how proud
he was of them and of her — seven children so
quickly that the house spilled over with them and
then two more. She saw them all small again, all
handsome and healthy except little Rosemary.

On that first night when her husband lies in his
grave a woman's memory remembers him young.
She cannot bear the night unless she thinks of him
young, the father of her children, the days when
they were still all together, and he was the provider
for them all.

Hyannis Port, at first only a summer home, had
become somehow their real home, though of course
they were never quite accepted there. One could
smile even into the darkness when she remembered
that meeting of the Hyannis Port Civic Association
— it was in 1951 — and her husband had listened so

patiently and in such heroic silence and when at last he spoke, in half a minute an old lady jumped up and broke in to tell the chairman that she hadn't come to listen to that "Johnny-come lately" make a speech and she stumped out.

Of course he had gone straight on, stopping only to laugh, because they had been coming to Hyannis Port then for twenty-five years. They had all learned to laugh. It had not been easy to be second-generation Irish in Hyannis Port. Really they had outgrown Hyannis Port, especially when they knew Jack was going to be the President of the United States. Oh, but that was years later — nineteen years later — and they had learned to love the seaport and its history, first of Indian lore and then of farmers and herdsmen and then of cod fishermen and the War of Independence and at last a town in its own right and a famous summer resort.

He — Joseph Patrick — had insisted that they all know the history of their hometown. Of course once he had made so much money people forgot about their being Irish. They bought their first big car — was it a Packard or a Cadillac? — anyway, the summers were fun, what with fan-tan and bridge and Ping-Pong. There had been some indecision as to whether they would choose Hyannis Port or Old Orchard Beach in Maine, but they had decided on the Cape — that was in 1925.

Three years they rented Malcolm Cottage — not a cottage but a huge rambling place — and

Joseph Patrick was so busy making his second million dollars that the family scarcely saw him all summer. He was there long enough to get very freckled, though, and on the fourth summer they had their own house, modeled by a Boston architect.

I was in Hyannis Port after the death of Joseph P. Kennedy, and it was revealing to discover how neighborly the people felt toward this big, sprawling family. They spoke gently of the father who had lived so many years in the dimness of illness and age, and they spoke of the days when the Kennedys were young. One local merchant said, "So many of 'em that it seemed like half the town come into my store when they trooped in thoo that door. What was they like? Just like other kids — laughin' and pushin'."

They had the first private sound motion picture in New England. That was when Joseph Patrick was interested in motion pictures — making much money, too — and Gloria Swanson came to visit them for a weekend. Any woman would have been jealous, for she was so petite, so pretty, so beautifully dressed, and she was married to the Marquis de la Falaise de la Coudray. She never went near the water, and she wrote her name on the wall of Kathleen's clubhouse, and the girls left it there for years.

By 1932 her last daughter and eighth child, Jean, had been born. Joseph Patrick was away so much, Rose had all the responsibility — no, not all, for his vivid presence was somehow always there.

Yet she had to be strong-willed and she had to learn how to be efficient — such things as a different color for each child's bathing suit so that when they all were in the water she'd know if one were missing.

While Joseph Patrick worked in Hollywood making his quick-selling pictures, she was what Jack called the "glue" that held the family together. She made them listen to her, too, and she talked about books and history and she was not above paddling any of them who disobeyed her — that was when they were small, of course.

Oh, those beautiful days when the children were all at home, the water carnivals and swimming meets, only the father would never allow more than one Kennedy in a category so they would not compete against each other. "Never come in second," he told them. "Second is just no good."

And wherever they went, he and she, they loved to have their children with them — at least a few, even one or two, if not more. Joseph Patrick wanted to be with all his children as much as he possibly could. He knew what they were up to, all the time — but he couldn't teach them to be good losers and he didn't try to. He wasn't a good loser himself. But he was brave and he taught the children to be brave.

Once the boys on shore saw an overturned boat in a rough sea, and they hurried into their own boat and made haste to save an all but drowning man. Young Joe was only twelve then and Jack was only ten. They never stopped to think of themselves. Young Joe need not have died so young, as he did later, if he had not volunteered in the war, after his own service was ended. But he was fearless, so strongly built, a shock of straight thick hair he could never keep brushed, bright blue eyes, always restless and doing something daring.

It was young Joe who helped his mother with the others and made and kept them a clan. He taught them to ride their bicycles, and to swim and play football until it became a family game, and tennis. Only Jack would not obey him and Joe had to fight him sometimes, always winning the fight physically for Jack was tall and thin and not strong. Joe never was able to change him, however much they fought. Yet the brothers loved each other and one day when Jack was older he said that if any of them ever amounted to anything, it would be because of Joe.

The boys had to finish school and they were at a fearfully untidy age. Jack's room, the maids complained, was always a mess of wet towels and swimming trunks and crumpled shoes and socks. As for shoe polish, at his graduation from Choate preparatory school his scuffed shoes showed under his graduation robe, the robe too short for his six-foot height. He was only sixty-fourth in a class of one hundred and twelve, and yet his classmates had voted him the senior most likely to succeed in whatever he chose to make his life. And he drew girls like bees to honey.

Her sons were often in mischief, Rose Kennedy had to admit. Once they even spent a night in jail.

It was at the Edgartown regatta, where the two older boys gave a victory party so wild that the management sent for the police. Both Joe and Jack were taken to jail, and their situation reported to the hired skipper of their yacht for bail. The skipper, a dour, positive character, stubborn but trusted by the father of the boys, refused bail, telling the boys they could stay where they were and learn a lesson.

———•—◆—◆—•———

Memories crowd the mind that first night when a woman lies alone in her bed while her mate lies under the sod.

In the summer of 1936 the children — only they were no longer children — were winning all the boat races. Jack, with Joe as coskipper, tied for the lead in the competition for star-class championship on the Atlantic Coast and collected two firsts in the July and August racing series. Eunice, skippering the *Tenovus,* with her sisters as crew, won time and again in the Wianno Junior class. When the races started she shouted joyously, ''All right now — everyone say a Hail Mary!''

And then the children were grown up entirely and, it seemed, so suddenly. Jack was running for senator from Massachusetts, and Eunice was out campaigning for him and telling people that her brother was ''firing the first shot against communism in this country.'' She and Pat looked beauti-

ful in their smart flaring skirts embroidered with
Jack's name and a picture of the Capitol building.
Their earrings were inscribed with the slogan
"Vote for Kennedy" — all very absurd, but touch-
ing and proving the old clan spirit that their father
and oldest brother had inculcated in them.

And then the year came when Joseph Patrick
was made ambassador to England and that was a
new life for them all . . . Memories, memories, and
not even death could wipe them away. But the rain
kept falling on the roof.

Three Kennedy women have had to live, or
exist, through that first night of the total realization
of death, which is, if I am to judge from life itself,
the first night when the beloved body lies under-
ground or in ashes. So long as even the body is visible, weakened though it may be, or even dead, it is
there. In the case of young Joe's death, there was no
body. It had been blown out of existence. He was
there high above the sea and in an instant he was
nowhere. But Rose Kennedy, and Jacqueline, and
Ethel, has had, each in her own way, to visualize,
against her will, that silent body in its lonely cell,
under the earth. Nothing and no one can prevent
the unseen sight. Only life can make it fade and,
even then, never quite away. Women whose loved
husbands die too young, however, deal differently
with the memory. One of the Kennedy cousins whom
I know has never returned to see a Kennedy grave,
to the vague reproach of friends and family.

"Why should I go? They are not there," she replies simply.

As for me, I went once to President Kennedy's grave, and will never go again. I remember him in other ways. But the Kennedy women, those whose husbands are in their graves, all visit those resting places. The two younger ones, I know, take their children with them. Understanding the deeply religious nature of Rose Kennedy, I surmise that she will do as her daughters-in-law have done.

But for Rose Kennedy I feel a special sympathy. Life is behind her. She is not a woman who lives through her children and grandchildren. She is too strong, too independent, too accustomed to a life of her own. She is accustomed, as well, to having been, and indeed to being, a beautiful woman.

Now no longer young, Rose Kennedy has only declining years to contemplate. True, they are also precious years in which music is more beautiful than ever to hear, art more significant, and the loveliness of nature more meaningful, because time is shortening.

The younger women, in contrast, her widowed daughters-in-law, have life ahead, years of life, and children to think of and plan for. Life is not theirs alone — it belongs to the next generation. There is an obligation not only to the dead husband but to the growing Kennedy family.

Outside my house the rain no longer falls upon the roof. It has changed to silent snow.

14

*T*HE LIFE of our nation has been changed by the Kennedy family. More than other families in American history, they have changed us. It is, of course, not only they. It is the timing of eternity. They came into prominence at exactly the right time in our national history and in world history. We were nearing the end of an age.

Two world wars and a depleting war in Korea had robbed us of many brilliant young men who would have been leaders in our national life and in the world. The greatest loss in war is never financial. The greatest loss is always and forever in the loss of brilliant young men and their capacity for leadership. We have had second-rate leaders both at home and abroad now for two generations.

Under the presidencies of Truman and Eisenhower people were only recuperating, were merely examining themselves and considering their problems. They did not as yet dare to face the future. They longed for guidance, for someone whom they could trust.

There was disappointment with the mildness of Eisenhower's period. He was highly respected for his military achievements, but he was obviously not experienced in political life, and, while his integrity and honesty were beyond question, his wisdom and preparation for political leadership were not. Nevertheless it was, I think, a good circumstance that we had the slow years, for they gave the people time to reflect, to take stock, to know their own needs, to formulate their search for a new way of life. This search has gradually crystallized into a deep desire for fresh thinking, for a new approach — in short, for heroes.

It was at this moment that the Kennedy men appeared. Had young Joe lived, he might have appeared too early and the Kennedy impact might have lost its effect. But John Kennedy arrived at the moment he was needed and in the way he was needed. He came with the power of the American tradition of immigrant origin but rich, successful, and powerful in three generations, and by his own actions and personality he appeared as the longed-for hero.

No one, to my knowledge, has ever made a study of what makes a hero. I do not mean the person who performs a brief brave action. Many people can be heroes temporarily when called upon for courage. I mean a man of heroic stature, who in all his doings and in his very being invites trust and confidence and finally adoration. Adoration is the result of what is called charisma. The best explanation of this often-used word today is its original Greek meaning — the "gift of grace."

I was discussing this yesterday at luncheon with a friend of independent political opinions. "Yes, and right there is the danger," he declared. "One Kennedy after the other in the White House and we would have a dynasty. First we'll have a Kennedy staying in the White House more than two terms because he knows how to make people love him. No, no — eight years is enough. I vote Republican every eight years, and Democratic in between. But you get a Kennedy in the White House with all his charisma and people get crazy about him and they'll want him to stay. And look at all these young Kennedys coming along! Don't you know some of them already see themselves in the White House?"

The Kennedy family has charisma, each member in varying degree but John Kennedy and his wife, Jacqueline, had it in superlative degree. Robert Kennedy had it also, and after his brother's assassination some of the dead President's charisma was given to him. It is not always composed of love. Sometimes it takes the form of violent hatred.

I was amazed one evening in Arizona when I happened to be dining at the home of an oil-wealthy widow, an honest-seeming, plain-appearing woman in her seventies. Another guest, a young man of high integrity and brilliant mind, happened to speak with admiration of Robert Kennedy and mentioned the possibility that he might be our next president. Instantly the amiable face of our hostess changed. Actually it became hideous with hatred.

"I wish someone would shoot him!" she exclaimed.

By coincidence it was only a short time before Robert Kennedy, too, was assassinated. But that evening an embarrassed silence fell upon us all. There is no logic in such hatred. One can only ignore it, and we spoke of other matters. Yet I could not but ponder such contrast of love and hate.

There is in our people, perhaps as a result of our national philosophy of democracy, a capacity for violence in love and in hatred such as I have not seen in any other of the many peoples I have known, except possibly the Koreans. The reason for this is not clear to me. Part of it is due, perhaps, to our inheritance from our ancestors. We are born of rebels and daredevils, and violent blood runs in our veins. Yes, I have lived among many peoples and have never known such violence as I see in my country — violent love, violent hatred. It is as dangerous to be loved here as it is to be hated, for in an instant this love can flash into hatred. To see a Kennedy clawed at, pawed over, and screamed at by frenzied adoring women is to shudder with fear. I know, for

I have myself been imprisoned in such a frantic crowd that I have had to be rescued by police. I am afraid of such love, for I know how a wrong word, a mistaken action, can change love to hatred.

But more than genes account for the violence in which we Americans indulge and which too many of us privately enjoy. There is a contradiction in our national philosophy that I have previously explored and need not here expatiate upon except to reiterate that it stems from dissatisfaction in individual achievement.

Hatred is, of course, one of the fruits of envy. I find envy a common fault among our people, the result of our system based upon competition and upon individual loneliness. How lonely Americans are, individually speaking! I find more lonely people in my own country than in any country I have ever known.

How many among us spend their evenings entirely alone, with only television for company! Television performers have infinitely greater influence than they could ever have achieved otherwise, and, I may add, far more than they usually deserve.

There is no doubt, of course, that television had much to do with building hero worship for the dynamically handsome Kennedys. Their fearlessness, their self-confidence, their youth, their idealism, the advantages of wealth and education appeared vividly upon the screen. Fortunately the young men were worthy of the attention they received, but television could have built them into heroes had they not been worthy.

We have only to remind ourselves of Adolf Hitler, that lowborn, ill-educated little man, who by the manipulation of those who created him and used him as a figurehead was able very nearly to destroy Europe. The German people have always been peculiarly susceptible to heroes. Land-pent as they are, a people of incredible industry of mind and body, aware of their own capacities and with a messiah complex toward other peoples, a handful of designing, powerful men created, as did the Israelites of old, a golden calf that they might satisfy their human need for a god to worship.

Such an event could scarcely take place in our country and in our times were it not for the unifying power of television. There upon a screen we all see the same face at the same time, we hear the same voice speaking the same words. We subject ourselves as a nation to the one man. True, we may also dislike him, we may as a nation reject him as we rejected Richard Nixon more than once, when he was his untrained self. Trained, however, by those who had cynically — or purposefully — studied the public mind, he was at last acceptable and accepted. Fortunately for us all and for the world, he is, I believe, a good man. But had he not been, the techniques would have been the same.

If television tends to unify, there are other forces that separate individuals from one another.

Age-old groups are breaking into division. As once the trade guild was the unit of industry, as later the trade union took its place, so now electronics takes the place of labor. Electronically we see the faces and listen to the voices of those we choose as hero. Electronically we hear news from all over the world. Without reading history or studying geography beyond high school, we learn superficially of clashes in the border regions of China and Russia. Without asking why there should be such as these, or why China overran Tibet, or why she fought a war to maintain her borders with India, we hear the news, the events that change our world, but which the news media never explain to us.

Because we know electronically the events that take place without understanding why they must occur, since there are inevitable and relentless reasons in the past for every event that is happening in the present, the young grow angry with their elders, their parents and teachers, and they show their distrust by rebelling in most obvious ways of dress and appearance, or of nudity and the flouting of control. They rebel but they express rebellion in low key, in indifference, in escape through drugs rather than drink.

The Kennedys illustrated the forces at work in our electronic age. They were dynamic but low-keyed. Their humor was edged with irony, even bitterness, and by thus expressing the mood of the young they became the heroes and the hope of the young. When they died a violent death, this violence, so anonymous, so senseless, expressed in another way the anger of the young. For the young, seemingly alike in their protest and rebellion, differ in their expression and sometimes they kill that which they long themselves to become and know they never can be.

Ours is an age of despair and revolt so deep that even individuals are pulling away from one another. Nowhere is this more evident than in our music, especially in our popular songs. At this very moment while I write I hear on the television a song which cries aloud in yearning pathos, "If that's all there is, then — let's go on dancing. Bring out the booze, and let's have a ball." And the list of titles of popular songs is repetitious individualism, touched with sad loneliness, "By Myself," "I've Gotta Be Me," "I Take a Lot of Pride in What I Am," "I'm All I've Got," "I'm Me," and so on infinitely.

This loneliness is significant, of course, as is the instinct to dance separately instead of together. But it is significant because this individualism, this loneliness, this separateness cannot be permanent. It is the prelude to a new grouping of human beings. And the likelihood is that the new grouping will be about an individual, the individual, who best understands and expresses the present mood of the young, who feel themselves not understood, who long to be understood, who will give themselves utterly to the one whom they believe understands, and he may then become a dictator. Never has our country been so ready for dictatorship as it is today.

Our leader, however, must be a product of our American tradition and idealism. For example, he must be a family man. A beautiful and faithful wife is an essential. She should not be in any sense his rival, but she should be suitably intelligent, preferably in a different field from his and preferably nonpolitical. She should never take precedence over him. Her presence should supplement his, but never surpass it.

In all these points President Kennedy was fortunate. His wife was beautiful, respectful of his position while maintaining her own position. It added to his own grace that he acknowledged with appreciation her ability to speak French and Spanish better than he could. He was proud of her artistic taste and gave her full credit for what she did to improve the appearance of the White House. It was as nearly an ideal combination as we have ever had in that august residence and they lived there with the ease of persons accustomed to luxury. Indeed, their personal accommodations were actually less luxurious than those to which they had been accustomed in their own home.

Had Kennedy lived, it is to be presumed that he would have had at least two terms in the White House, so long as he did not violate the requirements of the popular conception of what a hero should be. Perhaps his personal imagination might have transcended even these. That he would have been a brilliant and beneficent hero is certain. The danger would have been in his successes. Had this been Robert Kennedy, the brilliance and beneficence might have continued, although whether with the same wisdom we do not know.

One thing is certain. Americans today are weary of the extravagant, the overloud, the exaggerated, the "hard sell." They are tired of the political machine, the party organization. The cool, the soft-spoken approach, informed with wry humor, are now attractive traits.

Perhaps we are becoming more civilized — or perhaps we are only becoming more urbanized. We are no longer a rural people. Only 5 percent of our people are farmers and these are more than enough to feed the nation. All this has happened in a generation. It is no wonder there is a generation gap.

Parents and teachers have not had time or opportunity to keep ahead of the young people who were born even ten or twelve years ago. Teachers are hopelessly out of date with their knowledge and their pupils are ruthlessly cognizant of the fact that too often their teachers are unable to teach them and their parents not worthy of more than a sentimental impatient affection. They must find new people to learn from and to love.

Robert and his brother Ted and their families often came here to ski. If you ask a Vermonter "what they were like," he will pretend total indifference. Today, however, without questioning him, a Vermonter totally surprised me by reporting that one day when a photographer snapped a picture of Robert Kennedy on Stratton Mountain, Robert snatched the camera and smashed it. This he told me because at that instant an unexpected, and I must say unwelcome, photographer had suddenly appeared to take my picture.

"You sh'd smash it like Bobby did," my Vermont neighbor advised.

Alas, I had not so much courage! Have Robert's sons his courage? — for once again the Kennedys must look to the children as Joseph Patrick Kennedy did when he fell from grace. All the children hold potential power, for they all carry Kennedy genes, those whose fathers were and are Kennedy men and those whose mothers are Kennedy women. What will they make of their future? Much depends upon Edward Kennedy's decision concerning his own future. No decision has been made so far as the presidency goes, except that if he runs it will not be until 1976. Much remains in doubt even regarding that date or, indeed, any date.

He feels the heavy responsibility of the next generation. He has the reputed problem of his own life. Is Joan committed to him and to the Kennedy family? Few are the friends who can remain loyal under such circumstances. The few are the best treasure that life has to offer.

There will be total loyalty to Edward from the true Kennedys, of this I am sure. Those who do not have the Kennedy secret will fall away.

Whether or not Edward Kennedy chooses to run for the presidency someday, his position regarding the younger generation of the family remains difficult. They will have to grow up with the gossip, the scandalous talk. The older ones will already have read the newspapers and magazines. They are already aware of the shadow that has fallen upon the family. What will Edward Kennedy do to help them, first by winning their respect in his own right, and then by winning their love and loyalty?

First, if I may be permitted to advise, his influence can only have its full effect if he is completely honest with them. With those old enough to understand, he must be immediately honest, meeting every question fully and frankly.

The older ones can then help him with the younger ones. When the younger ones see that their older brothers and sisters respect Edward Kennedy and are willing to heed his advice and guidance, they will follow. Of course, they must be told everything in due course. I do not believe in shielding children from knowledge. Before others taunt them, and they will be taunted, they should know the truth. They should have it child by child, from Edward Kennedy, not only his own tragedy, but the tragedies that have befallen a great family.

Above all, they should know that they, too, will be haunted by the same tragedies: the tragedies of jealousy and envy and hate.

If I hold a grudge against my own beloved parents, it is that they, being persons of superior minds and loving hearts, reared me innocently in the belief that people are usually just and kind, unselfish and good. But I have had to learn by bitter experience not to expect justice or kindness, unselfishness or goodness.

I do not expect loyalty, for most people are not capable of loyalty and almost certainly not capable of loyalty if by being loyal they themselves are threatened. I have learned to be on Eve's side, not Adam's. Eve did well to persuade Adam to eat of the apple from the tree of the knowledge of good and evil. Eve was the wise one. She alone discerned the evil in the serpent and she alone taught Adam the truth — that evil exists, hateful, unrelenting evil, in the hearts of men and women who are serpents.

None know this as well as those of us who by nature love excellence, and for love of excellence are unsparing of ourselves and our talents. I hope and pray, therefore, that Edward Kennedy will teach the truth to that group of glorious children who are his children, his nephews, his nieces.

Of course, he must teach them, too, that there are some men and women who can be trusted for their goodness, but they are the few. Only the very few can be loved and trusted safely and without reservation. Yet the others, though they cannot be safely loved and trusted, need not be hated.

The superior person hates no one. Hate is in itself a corroding emotion, and the superior person does not stoop to it. It is quite possible, I find, to like and even to enjoy persons one cannot trust. I have friends — yes, I call them friends — with whom I can spend an enjoyable evening, but upon whom I would not bestow a single confidence, for I have eaten of the fruit of the tree of knowledge of good and evil.

My parents did not teach me. I had to learn by bitter experience not to expect anything of people — but how grateful I am when I am wrong about someone! And having found such a one, I never let him — or her — go. It is a treasure for a lifetime.

All this must be taught the Kennedy children. And among them may be some who have greatness in them; some who may again bring the Kennedy name to its height. They will suffer. They may even be killed. But in them may be that which is death to hide: talent.

And if, by reason of fear, one does not use his talent, if he hides it because he is afraid of his inferiors, then he will die, though he lives in the flesh. A true misery in life is to know that one possesses a talent which he has not the will or the courage to use to its fullest. However one is persecuted for his talent he must use it, if his spirit is equal to it.

Robert Kennedy's eldest son, Joe, is now seventeen years old. It was Joe who assumed the part of the honor guard at his father's funeral, who protected and comforted the younger children, who introduced himself to guests and shook hands and thanked them for coming, who stood at his mother's side at the burial, tears on his cheeks.

He was the one, too, who went to Europe with his uncle, Edward, and carried on the family tradition of courage by entering a bullfight in Spain, coming out bloodied enough to horrify his friends. He inherits the family grace as well, and already has presence of mind as a speaker. He shows great promise.

Robert, his younger brother, at fifteen has been twice to Africa on safari to take pictures of wild animals. He has a scientific mind, and little interest, as of now, in politics. He has a private menagerie of his own, including a honey bear, still half-wild, a huge tortoise, hamsters, parakeets, a raccoon, a pair of hawks, among other such inhabitants.

His younger brother, David, like most of the Kennedys, is interested mainly in sports. The others are scarcely out of babyhood. The new baby is Rory Elizabeth.

Robert Kennedy's home is empty without him, but his widow has devised a method of providing strong male influence for her many children by a schedule of visits from men who were friends of the dead father. In this way his children have not only adult male companionship, but that of brilliant men in the varied fields of art, business, science, and politics.

Of all the Kennedy women, none today has the strength and dynamism of Ethel Kennedy. None has the human warmth, and the spontaneity, the informality, and vivid understanding that Ethel Kennedy has. She is loved by the whole family — loved and admired.

Her first year of mourning is over. She has opened her house again to friends, especially to children. The first time was for a charity affair, where there was a pet show. She has set up a memorial to her husband — the Robert F. Kennedy Foundation. The proceeds will go toward the education of talented young people from underprivileged homes.

In a February, 1969, Gallup Poll, Ethel Kennedy was in first place as the most admired woman in the United States. Rose Kennedy came second.

Ethel has yet another quality appealing to the American public. She stands as a symbol of motherhood. Rose Kennedy had nine children, but Ethel Kennedy has eleven. And she has still another quite important advantage. She is not beautiful. Pleasant looking, healthy, vital, yes, but not beautiful, and therefore not a threat to other women. And the tragedy of her widowhood she has borne with such courage, such total lack of self-pity, that she deserves the admiration she wins.

It is highly possible, therefore, that a Kennedy woman, Ethel Kennedy, may become the new head of the Kennedy clan.

In addition to her own qualities for leadership, she has several handsome young sons, a situation remarkably similar to that of Rose Kennedy a generation ago. As a matter of fact, Ethel Kennedy's eldest son, Joseph Kennedy III, is only ten years younger than his uncle John Fitzgerald Kennedy was when he ran for his first political office.

The question now is, will Ethel Kennedy alone assume the double role of father and mother and urge *her* sons away from the competition of political life? Or will she continue the Kennedy tradition of fighting to win the highest post in the land?

Will the tragedies of the past determine the course of the third generation of Kennedys, so that the new Kennedy men themselves will set their feet upon the path that leads to the White House? Much, if not all, depends now upon a woman, a Kennedy wife, a Kennedy mother. But if Ethel Kennedy marries again, the course of our country could be changed.

I asked a friend if he thought Ethel might remarry. "She will certainly marry again," he insisted. "Oh, yes, of that I am sure. She has too much vitality, she doesn't like to be alone as a woman. Children don't count there. And people—the crowd, you know, who now adore her — will not demand of her what they demanded so cruelly of Jacqueline. You remember, she remained immolated, a sacrifice to sacred memory.

"The populace will take a devoted interest in Ethel's remarriage, every married woman will feel herself vindicated as a mother and housewife, and Ethel will have a happy life. Her emotions are not as deep as Jacqueline's, I'm sure. She can transfer herself more easily. Oh, yes — it will happen, I'd swear."

Another close male friend concurred. "She will marry again within two years," he assured me. "She is too much of a woman not to have a man around the house. No, I have no idea who he might be — but he sure has a tough act to follow. Bobby and Ethel were quite a team."

But it is possible, despite the convictions of friends, that Ethel Kennedy may never marry again. In that case she will remain the mainstay and leader of the Kennedy family.

Seven years ago, on October 1, *U.S. News and World Report* made the following comment:

"U.S. history shows no woman with three sons simultaneously holding high national office. Mrs. Rose Kennedy may be the first."

It is now possible that Ethel Kennedy will be the second.

. . . Are they haunted, these Kennedys?

Yes, but by greatness!